OUR APPROACH

to development has been shaped by the beliefs
and values of the faith we have held for more
than 1000 years. Firmly rooted in our tradition of
Mahayana Buddhism, the approach stresses not
material rewards, but individual development,
sanctity of life, compassion for others, respect
for nature, social harmony, and the importance
of compromise.
… (we want) to draw upon and conserve this
rich fund of social and cultural philosophy to
achieve a balance between the spiritual
and material aspects of life.

Jigme Singye Wangchuck,
the fourth Druk Gyalpo of Bhutan

WILHELM KLEIN
GÜNTER PFANNMÜLLER

Bhutan

Lustre Press
Roli Books

Looking at the captivating photographs in this book, I am reminded of how much Bhutan and Tibet have in common. We live in a similar natural environment, dominated by magnificent mountains, whose lower slopes are covered in thick forest. We have the same close relationship to the yak that encourages an inclination to a nomadic way of life. We eat the same staple food, *tsampa* or parched barley flour. Tibetan and Bhutanese ways of dress, while having their own distinct characteristics, are more comparable to each other than to the way people dress in either of our great neighbours, India and China.

We uphold the same Buddhist traditions and values. Splendid monasteries, temples and other monuments are a frequent sight in our landscape. For centuries, the monastic community has been the source of education and learning. And, although the Drukpa Kagyu that originated in Tibet has latterly become the major Buddhist tradition in the Land of the Dragon, it was the great Indian master Padmasambhava, fondly remembered as Guru Rinpoche, who firmly established Buddhism in both our countries.

These photographs reveal a country where little has changed and much has remained the same as it has for centuries. This is in contrast to what has happened in Tibet, where so much of our culture and natural environment have been destroyed and people's lives have been turned upside down. Nevertheless, the timeless tranquility that these images show is preserved in Bhutan gives me cause for hope. They recall how Tibet used to be and renew my dream that in the future, a genuinely autonomous Tibet will be an international sanctuary of nonviolence and good-will, where human beings and nature can live in peace and harmony.

16 April 2003

I

SPIRITUAL
LANDSCAPES

RINGED BY THE MIGHTY HIMALAYAS, Bhutan is a land imbued with spirituality. Landscapes speak their own language, a language that supersedes the spoken word. They have a life of their own and influence the behaviour of the people that inhabit it, inspiring their minds and colouring their souls. Once our ancestors had settled down, drawing sustenance from the land, they entered into a union with it and from this union sprang their particular identity. Adapted to a specific environment they became a reflection of the landscape, which mirrored itself in their facial features, in their beliefs, their demeanour and their deportment.

Whether they inhabited vast plains stretching to wide horizons, or narrow valleys fringed by towering mountains or undulating fields of golden wheat and paddy, the air people breathed and the soil they worked on impregnated them with the spirit of their land, making them reflect on that specific reality. They brought their homelands alive with deities and gods, with fairies, spirits, demons and ogres. Thus, there was no dividing line between the physical and the mental, between the rational and the emotional. In the spiritual form and matter became animated. Mind, body and soul were integrated in an indivisible oneness, which encompassed the land and its spirit. Animism thus, is not an antiquated religion; it was and is an existential experience, the lived truth at the core of our biographies.

The poetry of life rests in nature. Mystery and poetry do not survive when life is disengaged from nature. At best, life becomes measurable and a person's idiosyncrasies and identity become exchangeable. It loses its humane touch, its subtle uniqueness. Just as a film cannot transmit the soul-lifting fragrance of freshly cut grass or an individual's awe and humility when faced with the glory of creation, so does a permanent inhabitant of one of our modern mega-cities fail to empathize with the joy of people who see themselves as an extension of the land on which they live.

In the first light of dawn, our ancestors experienced nature's verdure as part of an eternal cycle in which they saw themselves as equal, not superior participants. Streams, brooks and forests created music even as storms roared threateningly over coasts and around sheer walls of rock and ice in the mountains. The sky was still called heaven and wielded supreme authority by blessing the land with warmth and rain, by causing fearsome thunder and by randomly flinging bolts of lightning. Solid and unmoving, mighty mountains were the sentinels of the gods and the sacred homes of divinities, as were rivers, lakes, forests and fields. Nature reminded our ancestors of their vulnerability while its ageless rhythm revealed that there was permanence beyond the individual's fragility. The soul of the earth was vibrantly experienced and everyone felt encompassed by it.

The demystified human being of today's modern world is barely able to communicate sensibly with those whose lives are still interwoven with this kind of magic. For people living in harmony with their surroundings, nature is an open book, narrating the ongoing story of life without the help of science; everyone, independent of the grade he has passed in school, can understand it. They are still amongst us, struggling to preserve their identity, struggling not to be overrun by the onslaught of a world that is determined by a set of ever so righteous scientific and socio-economic rules and a palette of philosophies.

This primordial relation of man and nature is still abundantly experienced in places where modern ideas have not yet penetrated deeply enough to rupture this natural synthesis. Bhutan, in the very heart of the southern Himalayas, is one such region. For the Bhutanese their land is alive. This is not the romantic perception of a city-bred mind but a feeling of oneness with the soul of the land as an outcome of daily labour and the struggle with nature, a part of a people's experience that is, as the saying goes, 'down to earth'. The interdependence of their actions and ideas with the world they live in is transparent; and where, in the past, it was not, mystery and religion stepped slowly in. Besides hardship, poetry and spirituality were part of everybody's daily life and not yet the reserved domain of literati, priests, or academics. Each landscape produced its own fables and extended fantasies in man's mind.

Mystic experiences and miracles were an undisputed part of their lives, the web connecting the physical with the spiritual. The sights, sounds, and fragrances of nature accompanied them constantly and transmitted a different essence of being than the one that is experienced in a modern, protected, urban environment, inducing humility, mystery and insights that have been lost to the purely rational mind.

Domesticating animals and plants did away with man's need to be permanently on the move. Settled in one place, his mind found peace. What once appeared threatening was now perceived as benevolent. Harnessing wind, water and fire, his practical mind entered a space where it could expand into the spiritual. That was when gods were born, when he gave artistic expression to the mystical, the incomprehensible. At one step further, philosophical systems evolved, comfortably absorbing these multifarious and polychromatic expressions.

In our modern worldview where only science and empiricism pass for truth, this ethos is seen as a product of the imagination. Already, in the first half of the twentieth century, Swiss psychiatrist and pioneer psychoanalyst C.G. Jung warned that a modern western interpretation of an alien knowledge-system must include the one-sidedness of its own position. Not doing so would lead to non-comprehension, a feeling of cultural superiority or reversibly, to naïve, unreflective acceptance. To

squash modern arrogance, he explained that in eastern imagination, the gods, fairies and demons that inhabit their lands, are equally present in the western psyche, in what he called the collective unconscious.

For the self-supporting Himalayan farmer and herder, life is still enveloped in the mystery of existence. It does not start with birth nor does it end with death. In a simple, saga-like fashion, the *Tibetan Book of the Dead*, the *Bardo Thödol*, is one of the treatises that has mesmerized some of the brightest western minds now for over two centuries. While western thought, still uncertain, fathoms a computational theory of the mind, the *Bardo Thödol* casts light on the fascinating question of what the individual's consciousness is. It also deals with the material body, feelings, perceptions, and karmic tendencies. It gives a specific answer to continuity within the overriding sphere of Absolute Reality, complementing the sense-based perceptions of natural sciences.

PREVIOUS PAGES 8–13
The Bhutanese concept of their identity relies emphatically on their spiritual heritage; the animistic origin of many of their beliefs make the Bhutanese ecologically aware participants in the theatre of nature. For them, all of nature is positively alive.

The Pristine World of the Himalayas: A journey into the Himalayas is a foray into a world that puts every thoughtful and inquisitive mind to test. It is not just the world of yesterday, a world of medieval living conditions as it is so often depicted and as a superficial survey would confirm it to be. Few such places and people have survived into the twenty-first century.

In the Himalayas, and especially in Bhutan, which has been spared the agonies of colonialism and social revolutions, a pristine world is still vibrantly alive. It is not dressed in the grey, plastic, and corrugated steel garb of the planet's underdeveloped regions. Most Bhutanese still follow a timeless combination of sacred and secular traditions that nourish more than the stomach, protect more than the bare body and create a spiritual well-being that cannot be substituted by materialism. This is not western imagination; it is the essence of their lives, in which the environment has fertilized their minds and in return they recognize the divine and pay reverence to it. It has left its mark in myths and legends, in customs and rituals, in astrology, poetry, song, dance and drama, in the values and norms of the people which epitomize the eternal struggle between the forces of good and evil.

Architecture reflects this aspect of life in Bhutan. Buildings such as dwellings stand as testimony to the artistic accomplishments of the Bhutanese. Built of carved and painted timber, they are supported by oblong blocks of limestone and granite. When constructing homes in rural regions and or when renovating the *dzongs*, their prodigious fortresses, not a single nail is used. Relying on techniques from the time before iron became readily available, they carve grooves on pillars and beams that sturdily support each other. These hardy habitations, their door-frames, beams and plastered walls, are alive with symbols and signs that span from simple animistic dragon and phallic symbols to abstract *mandala*s (cosmic diagrams), all of which impart a deep meaning in the lives of the Bhutanese. In their often isolated and secluded existence in far-removed locations, these symbols connect them with the outer world. They might live secluded lives, but they are not alone. They live under a spiritual roof, which they share with their ancestors and their neighbours, even though visiting people could often mean days of walking.

The *dzongs* that dominate the larger valleys of the country are more than religious centres. They also house the secular local administration and provide a focus and a grip on reality for a people encompassed by the solitude of primeval mountains. Their style, a mixture of sacred and profane architecture, was copied in the architecture of private buildings and influenced the national building code. For centuries, the dual system of administration reflected the parallel powers that

FACING PAGE 14
In 1637, when the *Shabdrung* camped where the Pu Chu and the Mu Chu meet, he had a dream that eventually resulted in the construction of the Punakha *dzong*. For 300 years, this *dzong* was the winter capital of the country. Recently, it was restored to its original grandeur and is experienced by the Bhutanese as the true heart of the country. During the cold months the *Je Khempo* moves here from Thimphu.

dominated their individual lives: the enigmatic and the mundane. Both occupy an equal space in their day-to-day judgements and the social and political environment. The experience of nature as bounteous or frugal and rough reappears in the personality of their gods and this duality is also seen in the political representatives that regulate their lives. Architecture thus mirrors and subtly influences the acceptance of the social system. The basic Buddhist tenet that everything is transitory makes itself felt in their building style as much as in their social behaviour.

The language of the Bhutanese, too, is ripe with expressions for the spiritual, giving way to shared phenomenal perceptions of reality that do not appear to the average western mind, which grasps concepts on a different level. For a Buddhist, who sees mundane existence as an illusionary game of the mind, an insubstantial transient experience, the sense of the word 'ignorance' differs sharply from how a westerner sees it, who only accepts knowledge if it falls within the boundary of science.

*Mantra*s (sacred utterances) can lead us to an understanding, even though the renowned British scholar L.A. Waddel, not hiding his western perspective, called them 'unmeaning gibberish' in his 1934 book on Lamaism (Tibetan Buddhism). The two syllables 'man' and 'tra' mean 'think' and 'support'. By uttering *mantras* and letting their sound vibrate through one's body, a stimulation takes place that opens a different perception than the one needed to solve a pressing problem or one that asks for immediate action.

The well-known *mantra 'Om Mani Padme Hum'*, uttered since more than a thousand years, innumerable times, all across the Himalayas by men walking across an inhospitable landscape, builds a bridge between the believer and his environment on a level of sound, vibration and intellect. He is aware that the sound emitted from his body mingles with the energy that surrounds him. Even though this *mantra* might not be the result of a discursive method of composition and evades a specific sensible content, it initiates awareness and a train of subtle thoughts that span from the meditative to the sharply intellectual. In Tibetan Buddhist culture, the meaning of each of the syllables of a *mantra* opens a door to a second layer of reality, representing and reminding an individual of the five other realms that surround him while he is moving across the physical world.

-OM-
removes the fear from the gods of being reborn

-MA-
extirpates the malignant spirits of the demons

-NI-
saves man from the pain of rebirth, aging, disease, and death

-PAD-
saves the hunted animals from the fear of pursuit and torture

-ME-
satisfies the hunger and thirst of spirits or *pretas*

-HUM-
destroys the pangs of suffering of those in hell

Meditating on the meaning of the syllables of the *mantra* is just one way of utilizing it. It helps to understand that the physical world presented by the senses is only one aspect of reality. Like an artist who already sees a different reality and experiences it while putting paint to canvas, like a composer who hears a string of notes that is not yet in the air, the spiritually trained mind perceives a quality in the environment that remains hidden to the righteous realist.

PREVIOUS PAGES 17–18
The Gasa *dzong* is the
remotest of the big *dzong*s in
Bhutan. It takes a two day up-
hill hike from the nearest
road junction to reach it.
Situated on a steep slope
underneath the 6395-metre
high triangle peak of the
Gangla Karchung, it is
reminiscent of the proverbial
Shangri-La.

FOLLOWING PAGES 19–21
One of the mightiest
fortresses in the Himalayas,
the Trongsa *dzong* stands at
the point where east and west
Bhutan meet. Until not too
long ago, the only road that
connects them passed
through the *dzong*'s
courtyard. The mighty gates
are still locked between
sunset and sunrise.

SPIRITUAL LANDSCAPES

There is no sharp division between the abstract and reality in Tantric thought. A blot of color is real, but at the same time it can also be a symbol that invokes a world of demons and deities.

More than a thousand years of continuous practice in monasteries, hermitages and temples has reinforced and solidified that perception. Through prayers and rituals, with the help of saints, *siddhi*s, lamas and hermits, an ever-renewing army of pious *gelongs* (monks) and religious effigies, the Himalayan people have upheld profound philosophical insights that are perceptible to the average farmer and herder. Depending on the depth of an individual's insight, the world is seen either as being inhabited by compassionate and wrathful deities or as the basic void behind all phenomena.

The Tantric Microcosm:
While the Near Eastern and the Mediterranean world took a monotheistic, mathematical-scientific path into the present; the people of India and the Himalayas continued their ancient spiritual journey. Until a short time ago, this spiritual journey also moulded most of East and Southeast Asia.

In western terms, we talk about different religions: Animism, Hinduism, Taoism, Jainism and Buddhism. For people following them, their tenets are the essence of their aggregated experiences. Their approach is akin to a westerner's vis-à-vis science for even though most westerners have never knowingly conducted any kind of scientific experiments themselves, they trust wholeheartedly in them. Every day, they experience the successful application of the principles of science, an experience that is not different to the Tantrist's who, for example, puts his trust in Avalokiteshvara, the deity, the incarnate idea of compassion and mercy. He is convinced and constantly reaffirmed that he will never be let down as long as he does his obeisance and abides with the innate rules that make up his world.

Few westerners ever touch the borderline where science's application becomes questionable, controversial, and debatable, especially where science and spirituality touch, where the mind meets the soul. This is where science fails and falls back onto a set of axioms, of prohibiting self-regulating principles, where it becomes fundamentalist, ending its relevance.

This is where Tantric Buddhism steps in and leads to greater depths. For the Tantric Buddhist there is no dividing line between the material and the spiritual world. Though he does not question the scientific approach and is as open as any westerner to its application, he does not subscribe to its innate restrictions. Like the true Christian, Jew, or Muslim, he does not need a mundane set of prohibiting rules; his spiritual awareness makes him fundamentally mindful and compassionate.

There is, however, an important difference. Contrary to a westerner, the animistic heritage of beliefs makes the Bhutanese an ecologically aware participant in the theatre of nature. For him, all of nature is positively alive

THE WORLD MANIFESTS

as the diversity of phenomena;
Do not perceive Samsara and Nirvana as two.
The nature of reality is beyond the limitations
of such categories.
So do not grasp at the parade of worldly things.
Everything partakes of the Clear Light.
Do not let your mind go chasing around,
For Deities are within you:
There is no need to search for them from without.
Understand that wisdom is innate:
Without any prayers, all Deities are inborn in you,
Without any effort, all the Paths and
Stages are attained.

Guru Rinpoche

and has to be respected; it is not just a plentiful depot of resources. Whereas most of the southern slopes of the Himalayas have been deforested during and in the wake of colonialism, the forests of Bhutan have largely been preserved in their original state. This respect for nature is even visible in such small details as banning the use of plastic bags and in the belief that the indiscriminate disposal of garbage would alienate the local deity.

Without demanding an ascetic lifestyle, Tibetan Buddhism allows the sensitive and reflective person to perceive the phenomenal world as illusory while it offers a set of morals that helps him navigate through his daily life without taking the joy out of it. Tantra gives substance and shapes to the invisible powers that control nature, life and death, making these powers palpably understandable to even the most untrained mind.

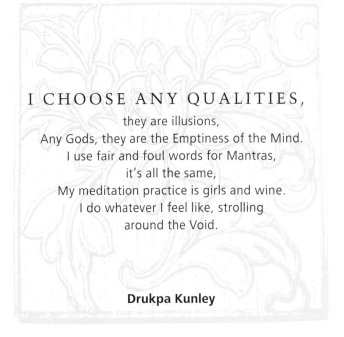

I CHOOSE ANY QUALITIES,
they are illusions,
Any Gods, they are the Emptiness of the Mind.
I use fair and foul words for Mantras,
it's all the same,
My meditation practice is girls and wine.
I do whatever I feel like, strolling
around the Void.

Drukpa Kunley

The symbolic world of Tantra, which easily offends a critical mind and is seen as the height of superstition, originated at a time when reading and writing as a means to communicate esoteric subjects were only accessible to a select group of people. By incorporating the soul-stirring poetry of a mystical language through *mantras* and the power of art as in *thangkas* (sacred scrolls), mighty images and the breathtaking swirls of mask dances, abstract subjects came within reach of the untrained mind. Today, these symbolic representations of a highly evolved philosophical system make up Bhutan's charm and beauty; they give a human touch to what remains largely incomprehensible to the person of the twenty-first century, biased by modern education.

In the words of Guru Rimpoche, the eighth-century founder of the Nyingmapa school, who is seen as the Second Buddha across the Himalayas, the wisdom and grace of the sages becomes a guideline for living. Contrary to Theravada (conservative Buddhism), Tantric Buddhism offers illumination and *nirvana* (liberation from suffering) during one's lifetime. It is not a promise of a better future in another life, but of a better and spiritually fulfilled life, here and now.

But the Tantric approach does not end at hallowed wisdom. Drukpa Kunley, the provocative fifteenth-century 'Mad Saint', the 'Divine Madman' who broke all formal rules of Buddhism and society, applied this wisdom in a most unusual and human way and is deeply revered for it. He is well known for his songs and legends and used ribald humour in his teachings to awaken the people to a higher awareness, free from conventional morality, self-obsession and hypocrisy. His words often sounded like the maxim of a nihilistic street-gang member in the abyss of any modern megapolis, but a perception of

Tantra gives substance and shapes
to the invisible powers that control
nature, life and death. It makes
these powers understandable to
even the most untrained mind.

To learn by heart is still the preferred way to teach and study. Together with a tutor, this boy is preparing himself for an examination.

Drukpa Kunley's deep spirituality and compassion, makes the difference between the materialistic and the Tantric existential concepts vividly alive.

Between the belief in the animistic deities of the ancient Bon religion and the Clear Light Vision of enlightened sages, the spiritual home of the Bhutanese is embedded in poetic expressions and manifestations that contain humankind's continuous biography in relation to nature. The Tantric existential feeling is beyond the materialistic, though it adheres to reason. As Buddha Shakyamuni said to his disciples: his teachings have to be tested in practice. There is a living thread across time, a thread that connects the individual with the teachings of the *siddhi*s, the lamas, and the Buddhas of the past. It keeps their insights alive and carries the experience of hundreds of generations, and of thousands of wise men whose lives were not much different from those of the contemporary Bhutanese. Even if modern-style life with its array of medical, chemical, biological and technical products offers more physical comfort, for a Bhutanese it cannot substitute the universe into which he was born. It cannot be a replacement for living in the grace of the sages' wisdom.

Dilgo Khyentse Rimpoche, the venerated Tibetan Buddhist teacher who died in 1991 and whose remains are buried in the district of Paro, came from a lineage of reincarnated teachers that leads in an unbroken line to the eighth-century Tibetan king, Trison Detsen. After an exceptional spiritual life, during which he once spent seven years in solitary retreat and later experienced the brutal occupation of Tibet by the Chinese, he explained the principles of the Tantric worldview in the Buddhist traditional manner, but in more modern poetic words.

Such a concept of reality is in stark contrast to the actively embraced western idea of material existence. In fact, what makes Bhutan so fascinating is the application of both of these worldviews, side by side, in a sensible manner.

High in the mountains, above 3500 metres, the yak-herders are still enmeshed in their ancient shamanistic Bon traditions. Though they call themselves Buddhist, their lives are woven around ever-present local deities and demons. In the agricultural valleys further down, the Tantric pantheon includes historical figures, bodhisattvas, saints, and sages. Lhakhangs (temples), gompas (monasteries – gonpa in Tibetan), and hermitages are seen all across the country. They are places of pilgrimage and prayer, visited to reinforce the traditional view of the universe. For every occasion, whether for the individual or society, there is a never-ending string of rituals, prayer meetings and offerings to benevolent or malevolent deities, while venerated lamas, Rimpoches, and tulkus (religious masters) live and teach in the unbroken tradition of one of the oldest religions in the world.

It is not easy for strangers to attend such ceremonies and gatherings for they would comprehend little of

SCHOLARS

and monks, you must consider my teachings carefully and experiment with them in practice: test their worth for yourselves and only if they prove their worth, then respect and practise them forever.

Buddha Shakyamuni

ALL PHENOMENA

of Samsara and Nirvana arise like a rainbow,
and like a rainbow they are devoid of any
tangible existence. Once you have realized the
true nature of reality, which is empty and at the
same time appears as the phenomenal world,
your mind will cease to be under the power of
delusion. If you know how to leave your
thoughts free to dissolve by themselves
as they arise, they will cross your mind
as a bird crosses the sky –
without leaving a trace.

Dilgo Khyentse Rinpoche

Nature in every manifestation is
alive for the Bhutanese. Air, water,
fire and earth are the classical
elements that create the space
where life can flourish.

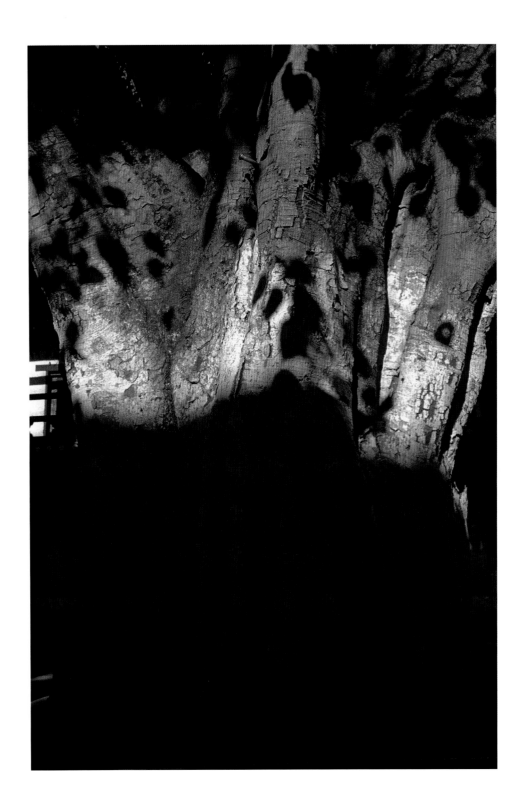

PAGE 30
'Whenever there is attachment in my mind And whenever there is the desire to be angry, I should not do anything, but remain like a piece of wood.'
Shantadeva

FACING PAGE 31
Prayer flags are testimony to the arrangement and the interaction between men and nature. They flutter on almost every prominent elevation throughout the country and dispatch their religious messages with the wind.

Prayer flags and Guru Rimpoche's image on the border pass of one of the old trading routes that lead from Bhutan to Tibet.

Generations of humble believers have prostrated in front of Padmasambhava. Their footprints have left impressive marks of a living religion and of piety.

what for the participants is the result of a lifetime of piety, of dedicated study, including years spent in retreat. For most foreigners, contact is limited to meeting modern Bhutanese who have studied in India or elsewhere abroad. These Bhutanese are the ones who are integrating the country successfully into the modern world while in their hearts they remain dedicated Tantric Buddhists.

Gross National Happiness:

What makes Bhutan such an outstanding place today, is the outcome of its unique history and living culture. While both, the Hindu and Tibetan Buddhist religions, had to face the onslaught and test of the modern world in India and Tibet, Bhutan remained enmeshed in ancient traits of thinking and communal behaviour. While elsewhere these have been radically adjusted to the forces of globalization that seem to stop at no place, secluded and shielded by towering mountains and raging rivers, Bhutan did not have to bow to global power players and is thus now able to modernize without destroying what has grown over millennia. Modern transport and communication took its time until new ideas could reach a country disconnected until a few decades ago from larger political entities. But now, as a member of the UN and several other international organizations, with TV, the internet, its Paro airport and its lateral road, the country cannot remain in spiritual and economic isolation anymore.

It was the fourth King, Jigme Singye Wangchuck, who realized that the profound difference between the western economic world view and the Tantric spiritual world view of most of his people were in basic contradiction. Having studied at both, Bhutanese monastic schools and at Western universities, he developed his idea of Gross National Happiness to balance the often ruthless forces in the pursuit of an ever-growing Gross National Product. It became the guiding line for his government and has now also become part of the new democratic constitution.

In retrospect it doesn't seem so revolutionary since most western nations have more or less developed social programs, but besides Bhutan, no nation defines the pursuit of national happiness versus the pursuit of the accumulation of national wealth as the principle that should guide its elected government. Mental and spiritual happiness are thus seen not only as part of the wealth a nation accumulates, but as the ultimate aim of every economic endeavour.

> MAINTAIN
>
> that state of simplicity. If you encounter happiness, success, prosperity, or other favourable conditions, consider them as dreams and illusions, and do not get attached to them. If you are stricken by illness, calumny, deprivation, or other physical and mental trials, do not let yourself get discouraged, but rekindle your compassion and generate the wish that though you are suffering, all beings' suffering may be exhausted. Whatever circumstances arise, do not plunge into either elation or misery, but stay free and comfortable, in unshakable serenity.'
>
> **Dilgo Khyentse Rimpoche**

II

LOFTY MOUNTAINS, DEEP RAVINES

'**THE PROSPECT BETWEEN** abrupt and lofty prominences is inconceivably grand; hills clothed to their very summits with trees, dark and deep glens, and the high tops of mountains lost in the clouds, constitute altogether a scene of extraordinary magnificence and sublimity.'

That is how Captain Turner, an early British envoy who reached the Punakha area in 1783, saw Bhutan. Even if one agreed with the analyst Peter Bishop, that 'travel does not so much discover worlds as create them', this visual impression is still an appropriate description of Bhutan that any modern visitor to the country could endorse. Most Bhutanese see their country through similar eyes.

Stretching over 46,500 square kilometres, Bhutan is about the size of Switzerland. But while one can cross Switzerland on one of its highways in two to three hours, it still takes three days of rough driving to cross Bhutan, even though its east-east west axis is not more than 300 kilometres as the crow flies and the distance from north to south does not exceed 170 kilometres. Within a distance of 100 kilometres, the country rises from 150 metres above sea level to more than 7000 metres, making it one of the most rugged terrains in the world, or as some call it, 'a steep staircase to heaven'.

Traversing the country before the lateral road was finished in the 1970s, took weeks if not months. Today, driving at a comfortable pace from Phuentsholing on India's West Bengal border to Thimphu, Bhutan's capital, takes about six hours. When the late Indian prime minister, Jawaharlal Nehru, made a state visit to Thimphu in 1958, four years before the road to India was finished in 1962, it took an arduous week-long journey along mule tracks through Sikkim, the Tibetan Chumbi valley and into the Himalayas to reach the Bhutanese capital.

While Bhutan stretches from east to west, the steep spurs that run south from the imposing Himalayas, which are divided by precipitous incisions of torrential rivers, define its rugged character. So, in the course of travelling from Thimphu in the west to Trashigang in the east, one is constantly driving up and down steep mountainsides while crossing several passes that are at a height of 3000 metres and more.

Towering over central Bhutan is the most prominent range, the Black Mountains, the dominant watershed between Bhutan's two major river systems, dividing the country into the eastern and western regions. Out of Bhutan's seven large rivers, some of them with 3000-metre deep valleys, the Mu Chu (Sankosh) and the Drangme Chu (Manas) flow through most of the country. The populations of eastern and western Bhutan hark from different backgrounds and adhere to different, though not antagonistic, schools of Buddhism, the Drukpa Kargyu in the west and the Nyingmapa in the east.

PAGES 38–41
Tiger Mountain, the 6794-metre high
Gangchey Ta 'who stretches his ears to
the sky', is one of the most beautiful
mountains at the border of Tibet.
Herders, most of the time young girls
from Laya, spend solitary summers in
this awe-inspiring environment.

Sprawling across southern Bhutan are the subtropical Duar plains, extending from the floodplains that fall within India. The Bhutan boundary begins several kilometres south of where the plains begin the ascent to the foothills of the Himalayas. These plains are Bhutan's greatest expanse of fertile flatland and its principal agricultural region. Where fields have not been carved out of the land, large tracts are thickly covered by savanna grass, bamboo, sal (*Shorea robusta*) forests, and dense, impenetrable jungle and teem with elephants, tigers, leopards, rhinoceros, deer, and wild buffalos. Bhutan's most important commercial centres, Phuentsholing, Gelephu and Samdrup Jongkhar, stand as sentinels at some of the eighteen Duars, the gateways to the Himalayas.

Densely wooded mountains rise sharply up from deep ravines as the plains, engraved by the force of fast-flowing rivers, cascades and waterfalls, ascends to the valleys of the Inner Himalaya, the heartland of Bhutan. It is home to its predominant inhabitants, the Ngalops and the Sharchops and it is here where we find Bhutan's cultural centres: Paro, Thimphu, Punakha, Trongsa, Bumthang, Mongar and Trashigang. Except for Punakha and Trashigang, these towns are all perched on slopes at a height of 2500 metres. Here, the widening valleys and the gentler slopes are extensively cultivated, but the people also farm narrow terraces intricately cut into steep hillsides. Moisture-laden southwest monsoon clouds bring revitalizing rain every summer after crossing the Bay of Bengal, while the High Himalayas in the north act as a shield against the icy Central Asian winds. The southwest monsoon breaks around mid-June and lasts until September, accounting for about eighty-five per cent of the annual rainfall.

Terraced fields, grass-covered slopes, and clusters of hamlets and villages are dotted with countless prayer flags that let the wind carry the Buddha's message. Together with a profusion of Buddhist *chorten* (Buddhist monument), *mani* (prayer) walls, and huge water-driven prayer wheels, they evoke the western vision of Shangri La. They assert that everyone, not only in the hallowed tradition of Buddhist saints, but equally so in modern analytic parlance, can 'create his own illusory world' while sharing a common environment.

Eighty per cent of Bhutan's population is engaged in subsistence farming, animal husbandry, and forestry. In the Inner Himalayas, the fertile alluvial soil of the valleys and the perpetual flow of water from the glacier-fed rivers permit growing of cereal crops, pulses, oilseeds, vegetables and last but not least, paddy, the staple food in all monsoon-dependent countries.

With an extended rainy season, two to three harvests a year are no exception in the sub-Himalayan foothills but the northern valleys can barely grow potatoes, buckwheat and barley during the very short summer. The mainstay of the semi-nomadic people living at and above the timberline is animal husbandry; they breed and herd cattle, sheep, yaks and zomos (a successful cross-breeding of yak and cattle). Butter and cheese are the main by-products, butter being consumed in huge quantities in tea. It is also used to shape sacrificial images for gompas and lhakhangs. Since motor roads are virtually non-existent here, horses and mules are bred for transportation, while chickens, pigs and goats are ubiquitous throughout the country.

High in the remote areas of the mountains roam wild animals such as the Blue Sheep, the elusive Snow Leopard, the Himalayan Black Bear, the Golden Langur, the Red Panda, the Musk Deer, the Takin (Bhutan's national animal) and the Black Necked Crane, to name just some of Bhutan's rare animals.

Buddhism has also left its traits here: except for self-defence and protection of their crops, hunting and killing of animals is prohibited in Bhutan. There are two wildlife sanctuaries in Bhutan, one at Manas in the south, and one at Laya in the north; both are remote and difficult to visit. The Manas sanctuary does have a tourist lodge in the middle of the forest, but both have yet to be opened for the public.

Abundant forests clothe the mountains and valleys of more than sixty per cent of Bhutan and a quarter of the land has been marked out as national parks or protected areas. The moderate climate at heights of between 1500 and 2500 metres encourages the growth of oak, maple and walnut, pine and conifer trees, followed further up by spruce, cypress, juniper, and dwarf bamboo. Even higher, at the timberline at about 4500 metres, birch flourishes. Lending colour to the slopes and meadows are exquisite rhododendrons, of which forty-eight different varieties have been identified in Bhutan. They grow from about 2000 metres up to 4200 metres, with some dwarf species at even higher altitudes. The vegetation above the timberline consists mostly of lush grassland. After the snow melts, this Alpine tundra turns into the luxuriant summer grazing ground for herds of yaks that roam these pastures up to an altitude of 5000 metres.

Before the 1959 invasion of Tibet by the Chinese People's Liberation Army, most of the northern region transacted with Tibet, using age-old trade routes leading to Lhasa. Spices and cloth from India, tea and grains found their ready market in the Tibetan capital while wool, black salt and yaks were brought down from the Tibetan plateau. The four mountain passes that were once witness to the movements of hordes of people are now deserted, a consequence of the invasion of Tibet and a vague Chinese claim of suzerainty that resurfaced after China published a map in 1961 showing alterations of the traditional borders in Beijing's favour. Bhutan then closed its northern borders and redirected its entire outlook and trade towards India. The yak-herders at the border, though, still slip across it occasionally and many of them have visited Gyantse or Lhasa.

FACING PAGE 42
Gnarled and rugged trees mark the upper line of the forests. Monsoonal storms and icy winters have given them their often bizarre fairyland forms.

FACING PAGE 44
Crossing Bhutan from west
to east, the road winds
through several passes at an
altitude of 3000 to 4000
metres. At this height, the
lush vegetation of the valleys
gives way to luxuriant high-
alpine flora.

PAGE 45
The Mu Chu, where it leaves
its icy source and enters the
upper tree line.

The country's rich biodiversity is one of its outstanding assets. In prehistoric times, Bhutan was already known as Lhojong Menjong, 'the southern country of medicinal herbs' and it is today one of the pharmaceutical industry's most promising regions for scientific bio-prospecting. Most of the population still depends on drugs developed by indigenous methods from herbs and plants that grow at high, sun-drenched altitudes.

As the mountains rise higher from the Duars to the glaciers along the Tibetan border, all the climatic zones of the earth, from sub-tropical to arctic, are discernable. In the past, most domestic communication and trade in central and eastern Bhutan took place within north to south running valleys, each valley a world unto itself close to the mysterious Shangri-La westerners had conjured up. It was often the case, for example, that a dialect spoken in one valley was incomprehensible elsewhere. The new motor road that traverses these valleys and several 3000-metre high ridges from east to west, has speedily, within a generation, unified people that had rarely left their self-contained world before.

An age-old network of paths and mule tracks cross an endless number of rivers and creeks with rope and suspension bridges or mere logs, intersecting the country and connecting its 4500 rural settlements and twenty *dzongkhags* (districts). Travelling north from Bhutan's population centres towards the High Himalayas and the Tibetan border can still only be done on foot because mountains soar to more than 3000 metres in this area, which consists of forty-five per cent of the country's surface. The most remote villages like Thanza at 4800 metres and Laya at 3860 metres can only be reached after days of exhausting treks. The majority of the population lives more than half a day's walk from the nearest motor road.

PAGES 46–47
Lobeysa is a little village on the way to Punakha. It houses the famous Chime Lhakhang where barren women from all over the country come to pray for offspring. It was here that the 'Divine Madman', Drukpa Kunley, built a *chorten* at the end of the fifteenth century.

Sparkling white glaciers cover ten per cent of the country's total surface area but, surprisingly, there are no glaciers in the Inner Himalayan ranges – they are all found in the arc of glaciated mountains along the Tibetan border. Several peaks are higher than 7000 metres; the highest, Kula Gangri, reaches 7554 metres and Bhutan's sacred Jomolhari, 7320 metres. For the Bhutanese, their highest peaks are not just any mountains. Kula Gangri represents Kuvera, the king of the Tibetan mountain demons, while Jomolhari, the home of Tsheringma, one of Bhutan's most revered mountain deities, stands like a sentinel above Tibet's Chumbi valley, the erstwhile southern gate to Lhasa. Ascending them is now prohibited in the belief that any intrusion could infuriate Kuvera or Tsheringma. Minor disturbances of a deity's serenity have caused landslides and flash floods in the past, which happened when an expedition was on its way to the Jichu Drakye in 1983. Since then, the scaling of all sacred mountains is officially discouraged.

Lieutenant Chahu, a modern Bhutanese officer and member of the 1970 Indo-Bhutanese expedition that climbed Jomolhari before the decree came into effect, did not make it to the top even then. After a cruelly exhausting ascent and within reach of being the first Bhutanese to scale the most sacred of Bhutanese mountains, he stopped 30 metres below the peak. Later he explained:

'I looked up towards the seat of the Goddess Tsheringma and something happened to me. I felt that I could not go up to the top. I was too steeped in the traditions of my country to break with them so suddenly.'

Lieutenant Chahu, as modern as he is, perfectly represents the Bhutanese mindset, one that is oriented less towards accomplishment and more towards being in concordance with the traditional values that shape the lives of the people.

The inhabitants of the Greater Himalaya live in an intimate union with nature. For them the mountains, especially those peaks that are covered with eternal snow, are the seats of the gods. These gods can be pleasing or wrathful, and, according to the specific deity, the Bhutanese revere mountains as both benevolent or malevolent forces of nature. In their solitary, remote location at the utmost edge of possible human habitation, the Bhutanese remain acutely aware of the individual's fleeting existence, his place in nature, and his vulnerability before the eternal grandeur of the Himalayas. What a westerner vaguely calls divine, has for

them names and shapes, and is accessed and propitiated by consideration, compassion, and obeisance.

PREVIOUS PAGES 49–52

Perched at a height of 4000 metres altitude, Laya is one of Bhutan's most remote villages. It is another two days walk from Gasa. 50 years ago, it was on the mule trek from Punakha to Gyantse. Now, since the border is closed, it is at the end of a long arduous climb, nestled beneath the icy barrier that divides Bhutan and Tibet.

PAGES 53

After a frugal breakfast, these young students have a few more minutes to warm up in the early sunlight before they return to their studies, to endless hours of repetitions of sacred texts, which they have to learn by heart.

When the flags flap in the wind, prayers are carried through mountains, valleys and across the globe. Like the praying wheels, prayer flags are poetry in motion.

III

SPIRITS, GODS
AND
DIVINE KINGSHIP

KNOWINGLY OR UNKNOWINGLY, every culture rests at the apex of a world of commonly shared memories, of proven facts, historical narratives and records, oral traditions, legends and sagas. The more factual and pragmatic a culture becomes, the deeper their ancient messages are buried, revealing themselves in unintelligible beliefs, in strange fears and unusual behavioural patterns. The entire set of ethics and morals that guide a people can be traced back to prehistoric myths and their development. They appear in many layers – regional, national, ethnic, and religious – and more often than not, have been interwoven over millennia.

The Himalayas were a creative ground for this kind of cross-fertilization. The Central Asian myths of pastoral herdsmen and the Indo-Aryan myths of settled agriculturalists mingled on the Tibetan plateau. Due to the topography and the nearness of extreme climatic zones, the idiosyncrasies of people of such different lifestyles as those who lived in a lush tropical environment or in the freezing plains of Tartary, faced each other on the fringe of the Tibetan tableland. There were others: the herders from the rocky deserts of high Alpine regions, and hunters and gatherers from confined valleys and forests. They all contributed to the peculiar set of beliefs that evolved in the pre-Buddhist Himalayas and which still thrive there today in a syncretic form.

The local tribes, as most people between Siberia and the Ganges delta, were polytheists with a strong shamanistic tradition. In Tibet, this evolved into the Bon religion with a vast pantheon of gods and spirits and a plethora of rituals. As the mouthpiece of the spirits, the Bon priest, the shaman, occupied a special position in society.

In prehistoric times, our ancestors shared one thing in common: an awe of nature. This awe, amounting to veneration, is also the predominant theme of Himalayan myths and folklore. First, natural entities were deified, and then, as we know from legends, the gods came down to earth and Divine Kingship was born.

There are several such legends that tell us of the divine origin of kingship. In the Kashmir version of the *Gesar Saga* (a secular Tibetan text depicting the adventures of Gesar, a king and magic hero), a headman helped a god fighting the devil Curulugu and as a boon, he asked the god to send one of his three sons to become the king of his country. The son descended by a supernatural rope, which remained attached and curled on the crown of his head. This led to the belief that once a crown prince was born and had learned to ride a horse at the age of thirteen, the king had to return to heaven the same way he had come.

With the wide acceptance of the divine origin of the kings, the first step from a tribal based shamanistic

A caravan on its way to Laya. Men and unburdened beasts rest on a sunbathed meadow.

FACING PAGE 60

When the monsoon drives in
the moisture-laden clouds
from the Bay of Bengal, the
forested slopes of Bhutan's
mountains disappear behind a
veil of dampness.

PAGE 61

An early morning in Merak.
Without sun, it can be damp
and cold in the mountains.
It takes sturdy people to
make their homes in such a
difficult environment. The
Brokpas of Merak, herders
and agriculturists of Tibetan
stock, have known no other
life and have no urge to move
down into the valleys.

society to a stratified society based on secular law had been taken. The names of the sons of Trigum, ruler of Tibet, point to that direction. They were Shatri (administrator), Nyatri (leader) and Chatri (warrior). They also indicate an Indian yogic origin of the myths, including the departure of the soul through the highest *chakra* (nerve centre of spiritual energy), on top of the head. The incorporation of this idea into the *Bardo Thödol*, the individual soul's search for a new incarnation, though, is of local Tibetan origin. It later became basic to the acceptance of reincarnated lamas.

After the advent of Buddhism in the second half of the first millennium, the sense of compassion and non-violence slowly prevailed over cruel Bon practices. The belief in the kings' divine origin was given up. Now the lamas held the reins of spiritual authority and they, in time, also acquired temporal power. This lasted until the seventeenth century. Though Bhutan always existed as a separate geographic entity and was influenced by Buddhism since the eighth century, we cannot speak of any national Bhutanese history until then, since the country, locked as it was within inscrutable mountains, was rather inaccessible and divided into small kingdoms, principalities, and fiefs.

The developments in Tibet cast their shadow on the greater region to the south of the Tibetan plateau. It was then known as Lho Yul, the southern country or later as Lho Mon, the dark country, that had not yet heard the word of the Buddha.

Buddhism Enters Tibet and Bhutan: During the first half of the first millennium AD, Buddhism went through a fundamental change. The original Hinayana doctrine had focused on the individual's salvation and abhorred sacrifices, excessive rituals and the belief in a pantheon of gods. Over the centuries, after Buddha's death, his *Parinirvana* (ca. 480 BC), it veered more towards a monastic way of life. It could not really compete with the polychromatic attraction Hinduism had where *'bhakti'*, the devotional love of god, touched the hearts of people. Buddhism's pivotal philosophical doctrine turned out to be too demanding for people who were still steeped in superstitions.

FACING PAGE 63
A *tshechu* performance at the Gantey gompa. This annual dance festival revives the ceremonies, movements and sounds of Pema Lingpa's time. Pema Trinley, his grandson, founded this, the country's largest Nyingmapa monastery and the only Nyingmapa foothold west of the Pele La, the pass that divides eastern and western Bhutan. The Gantey *tulku*, the ninth reincarnation of Pema Lingpa resides here and is equally revered by Nyingmapa as by Drukpa disciples.

It took several Buddhist councils over a period of six hundred years until the original creed appeared in its new garb as Mahayana Buddhism in which Buddhist, Hindu and animistic traits were syncretized. Asvaghosa, the eminent Sanskrit poet and scholar brought the concept of the eternal soul back into Buddhism – even Lord Buddha's doctrine of dependent origination, the law of causation, had been watered down. Once it was

widely accepted, Bon and Hindu rituals found their place in an otherwise stringent philosophy.

Sir Charles Bell, an authority on Lamaism who spent twelve years as a diplomat with Tibetans and was an early resident in Lhasa, observed this development critically:

'How greatly this religion differed from the teachings of the founder! The doctrine of salvation by faith instead of by work, the belief in supernatural beings, the reliance on images, ritual and charms and the abstruse metaphysical discussions, all these were fundamental departures from the life as lived, from the words as spoken, by the Buddha himself.'

The eminent Indian scholar Dr B. Chakravarti, though, saw it differently: 'If the people fail to realize the truth as principle, they may easily understand it as personality, that is, in a personified way. They will gradually realize the truth as a principle after they have known it in a personified way.'

The history of the Himalayan people, their gradual switchover from being known as some of the most savage tribes that inhabited the earth to pious and compassionate men could only happen through a slow process of syncretism. The heart of Buddhist teachings has never been compromised and it still lives on in the essential teachings of Rimpoches, *tulkus*, and lamas.

How this happened and and how it influenced the people of Bhutan is connected with three names: Guru Rimpoche, Pema Lingpa, and Shabdrung (title meaning 'at whose feet one submits') Ngawang Namgyal, considered the founder of Bhutan. It is a fascinating story and contains the essence of what today shapes the devout attitude of the Tibetan and Bhutanese people.

In the Himalayas, history and religion cannot be divided. Every new insight into the philosophical matrix of Buddhist thought influenced the history of the region. The power of the mind and the power of the sword entered into an inseparable unity and dependence.

FACING PAGE 64
Students rushing up the stairs of the Trongsa *dzong* to their evening prayer meeting.

Subduing the Forces of Evil: Guru Rimpoche, also known as Padmasambhava, brought Buddhism to Tibet. For the Himalayan people he is the Second Buddha, the saint who rescued them from ignorance, who ended the Dark Age, subdued the evil spirits that terrorized them and brought relief to a people haunted by fears and superstition. He is also known as Ugyen Rimpoche, Ugyen Padma Jungne and Guru Padma. He is the Lotus Born.

The kind of Buddhism that reached Tibet around the middle of the first millennium AD was a mixture of Mahayana, aboriginal beliefs, and Tantra. A Bon tradition tells us that during the fourth century, a chest with sacred Buddhist scriptures fell from heaven and initiated the advent of the new creed. But the *Blue Treasury of Records*, the Tibetan annals, confirm that the Indian Pandit Losemtso and the translator Litese were the ones who actually brought these holy books.

The southern country, so called from a Tibetan point of view, was at that time an outlying part of Kamarupa, an ancient Indian kingdom whose centre was in Assam. From a stupa erected in Kashmir in the fifth century, we know that its king had a Buddhist preceptor named Stonpa, who came from Lho Yul, which hints at an even earlier, though not significant presence of Buddhism in Bhutan. A similar situation existed in Tibet. The abstract teachings of Indian Pandits who visited Lhasa in the early days could not reach the people's minds and it took the coming of Guru Rimpoche to change the situation.

Today's visitor to Tibet or Bhutan is continually confronted with fear-and-horror-striking images that, however, are not what they seem to be. In a perfect syncretizing process, Padmasambhava brought the Bon deities and demons into the Buddhist world and removed superstitious fears. At the same time, he instilled the main theme of Mahayana Buddhism, compassion and love, in the minds of people.

What happened in Tibet during the eighth and consecutive centuries is what we would see today as a cultural revolution. The conservative Bon elements in society did not give up easily and centuries of political turmoil followed.

On Padmasambhava's return to India, he stopped at the court of his disciple, King Nawoche, who was in conflict with King Sindhuraja of Bumthang. Sindhuraja had lost his son, a brave warrior, during the fighting and did not have the will to live any longer. He lost faith in the deities and soon fell seriously ill. On invitation, Padmasambhava came to Bumthang, in today's central Bhutan to cure the king of his spiritual sickness. He converted Sindhuraja to Buddhism and negotiated peace between him and King Nawoche. Then he commenced his teaching, trying to rid people of superstition, just as he had already done in Tibet.

FACING PAGE 67
To teach is an act of compassion. To help someone overcome ignorance and assist him on his path leading to deliverance produces good karma. Being a teacher in a Bhutanese monastery follows a different calling than the ethics that guide professional western education.

Subduing spirits was what people understood, it was their world, the world they experienced realistically. For a modern person this remains a strange idea, but for the people who lived then, demons and ogres had a physical reality. Their minds were haunted by them and in this context, the Guru's actions can be compared to a modern psychoanalyst's. Today, Guru Rimpoche's sojourn in Bumthang is seen as the beginning of the Bhutanese Buddhist era.

Consequently, the century-old dilapidated Kyichu lhakhang and the Jampe lhakhang, two of the 108

PAGE 68
Two students testing the sound of their trumpets. The sonorous music enters every room in the gompa, adding a special sentiment to the ambience of a secluded religious life.

PAGE 69
Designing a sand *mandala* is an art and an educational experience for the students. After days of meticulous work, it is then recklessly destroyed in an instant, just as life itself ends suddenly. Impermanence is thus experienced practically, not merely as an abstract idea.

temples which Songtsen Gampo, the king of Tibet, built after AD 642, were renovated and the construction of a series of monasteries begun.

It is today's Bumthang and Paro that have become the religious centres of Bhutan. Over the centuries, an infinite number of legends were woven around each of the ancient gompas, lhakhangs and hermitages, which were and still are the home of revered lamas and Rimpoches.

The political turmoil in Tibet between the ninth and the twelfth centuries, combined with the advent of Lamaist sects and the ensuing conflicts between them had considerable consequences for Bhutan. A never-ending stream of expelled monks, followed by armed incursions, found their way south into the valleys of Mon Yul, which in the meantime had become a fertile ground for disseminating the new creed.

The intensified philosophical discourse created several schools and sub-schools, out of which grew the four major traditions of Tibetan Buddhism:

The Gelugpa, the Lamaist sect, best known worldwide also as Yellow Hats, whose spiritual head, the Dalai Lama is seen as a reincarnation of Avalokiteshvara.

The Sakyapa whose main deity is Manjusri, the Bodhisattva of Wisdom.

The Nyingmapa, the sect that is also found in eastern Bhutan and whose principal saint is Guru Rimpoche.

The Kargyupa. One of its sub-sects, that follow Drukpa Kargyupa's teachings, became the state religion of Bhutan.

All these sects teach the same creed and differ only in minor points: their saints, their dress, their symbols, and their ritual practice.

FACING PAGE 70
Keeping the butter candles burning is one of the duties of monk students. The ancient wall paintings and inscriptions carry messages that are as ancient as the religion. Nothing has changed; no new ideas have entered this chapel since the great-grandfather of the *Shabdrung* laid the foundation of the Trongsa *dzong* back in 1543.

While Nyingmapa (*pa* means sect) is known as the unreformed sect with a strong Bon tradition, Gelugpa is known as the reformed sect and the Sakyapa and Kargyupa are semi-reformed.

***Tertons* – The Treasure Revealers of Bhutan:** When Padmasambhava established the Nyingmapa, he already planned for the development of the creed in the future. He buried certain religious 'treasures', scriptures and other material and prophesized where, when and by whom they would be found. He knew that the time was not yet ripe to disclose the more subtle and demanding concepts and that the religion would need some fresh impetus from time to time, hundreds of years after its foundation.

Subsequently, according to the doctrine, about 1000 minor, 100 major and five sovereign *Tertons* (Treasure Revealers) appeared between the twelfth century and today. The last of the sovereign *Tertons* lived just 100 years ago; some are active amongst us, and others are expected to reveal themselves in the future.

The heart of the doctrine can be understood by the life of the most outstanding *Terton*, the saint Pema Lingpa. In Buddhist thought, we must distinguish between two lineages, the spiritual lineage, the one along which rebirths happen and the physical lineage, which is a person's genealogy.

As we know from the *Thangyig Sheldrakma*, a biography of Guru Rimpoche, which was supposedly written in the thirteenth century, King Trison Detsen's beloved daughter Lhacham Padmasel, 'The Bright Lotus', suddenly died. The Guru who was in Tibet at the time said: 'Do not be sad, along some "pure" and some "impure" lives, she will be reborn as the *Tertons* Padmaledretsel, Drime Wozer, and as Ugyen Pema Lingpa who will reveal the Treasure in the Burning Lake.'

Pema Lingpa was born in 1450 AD into a family of Bumthang blacksmiths, a trade he also took up when he was nine years old. His autobiography tells us that in his twenties, he discovered his first *Terma* (Spiritual Treasure), a casket with script rolls that seemed to be unreadable, but actually contained the 'Quintessence of Secrets'. With these, he retired to the Mani gompa where he fell into a trance and learned to decipher the script. He became enlightened and started to preach Buddhism, revealed many more treasures and founded several monasteries during his life. Of all his discoveries, the one at Mebarthso, the 'Burning Lake' in Bumthang, is the best known and every Bhutanese child has heard the story just as certain Christian stories are common knowledge in the west. The story goes that Pema Lingpa dived with a lighted butter lamp into the lake after telling onlookers that his lamp would be extinguished if he was a false spirit. He vanished in the dark water, but then resurfaced after a while, with his butter lamp still burning brightly and a new sacred text in his hand.

Pema Lingpa travelled widely and soon had many disciples even though he never had studied any scriptures and had acquired wisdom apparently without effort. His entire life seems to have been filled with an uninterrupted flow of intuitive knowledge, miraculous powers, and prophetic abilities. His mystic visit to Zangdokpelri, the rainbow-hidden heavenly abode and ultimate seat of the great Guru, brought the description of the Buddhist paradise to Bhutan. It is now recreated in the mask dances he choreographed during his lifetime. They are still performed according to his instructions during Bhutan's religious festivals.

All Lamaist sects in the Himalayas revere him greatly even though his preaching was along the lines of the

Nyingmapa religious doctrine. His appearance invigorated Buddhism and today he is the best known *Terton* and saint in Bhutan.

Building the Nation: Drukpa, one of the four sub-sects of Kargyupa, belongs to a tradition of oral transmissions starting with Lingrepa Pema Dorji (1128–88) and Tsangpa Gyare Yeshi Dorji (1160–1210), the founder of several monasteries, such as the Ralung monastery. While a thunderstorm was raging during one of the constructions, Yeshi Dorji saw a huge dragon (*druk)* in the sky. This gave the name to the sect and to Bhutan itself, which for its inhabitants is known as Druk Yul, the country of the Thunder Dragon. The Ralung monastic complex in Tibet was the centre of the Drukpa school and was ruled by a hereditary line of Gya prince-abbots. One of the students, later known as Lama Phajo (1184–1251), came to Bhutan where he built the Cheri monastery, the first Bhutanese Drukpa monastery in the valley of Thimphu. When he died in 1251, the sect was already well established in western Bhutan. Many of the country's aristocratic families claim their descent from him.

A variety of Tibetan sects and sub-sects tried to establish their dominance in Mon Yul, but until the seventeenth century, none of them prevailed. It took a succession struggle between two opposing incarnations of Kunkhen Pema Karpo at Ralung to change the situation. Following a prediction and a dream, Ngawang Namgyal (1594–1651), the founder of Bhutan, left Ralung in 1616 at the age of twenty-two when his opponent ascended the Hierarch's throne. Ngawang Namgyal, later characterized by his white beard, was charismatic and gifted with a decisive character.

By 1656, shortly after his death, the political superiority of the Drukpas in western and eastern Bhutan was irreversibly established, even though the Nyingmapa remained the dominant Lamaist sect in the east. But before this could happen, the *Shabdrung* had to defeat the army of the Tsang Desi (elected temporal ruler) that followed him to Bhutan. In a rebutting letter, which the Shabdrung sent to the quasi-omnipotent Desi, he wrote:

'…Now, if I cannot destroy you and your family completely, then it means that Drukpa does not have protective deities. In particular, it would then be certain that I am not the incarnation of Kunkhen Pema Karpo and I do not belong to the noble lineage of Drukpa.'

According to legend, a war of black magic followed, during which the Desi summoned an army of black magicians to destroy the Shabdrung. But his strategy was in vain for soon after, both the Desi and his wife died of smallpox in 1621 and the Shabdrung's magical powers and especially the power of his protective deities were soon recognized and respected across the entire Himalayas. Today, they are one of the main

FACING PAGE 74
Objects and tools in a mendicant's life have symbolic meanings. The bell, for instance, signifies the emptiness, inherent in all phenomena.

psychological columns on which the modern theocratic nation rests.

The Shabdrung as Ngawang Namgyal became known, was a nation-builder. He initiated administrative control, had impenetrable *dzongs* built at strategic points of the country and formalized a written code of law, the *Tsa Yig*, based on Songtsen Gampo's seventh-century religious and worldly edicts. It had three objectives: the contentment of the people, the proper influence of, and respect, for authorities and the support of the *sangha* (Buddhist monastic order). It prohibited the taking of life and fined homicide with blood money. Robbery was fined with a hundred-fold repayment if it was committed against the church, eighty-fold against the king and eight-fold against ordinary subjects. Fines were also imposed for adultery and falsehood put the offender to oath in a temple with dire consequences from the deities and gods if he was perceived to be insincere.

But the most consequential change that influenced the ensuing two centuries was the promulgation of the dual system of government, the separation of the religious and the secular. While western thought at the time already focused on the separation of legislative, judicative, and executive powers, the modernization of Bhutan meant a clear distinction between the individually experienced spiritual and the indispensable mundane matters of the world. The Je Khempo was the head of the religious system and responsible for the *sangha* and the religious ceremonies. The Desi (the *Deb Raja*, the civil ruler) held political power. He had to collect taxes, raise labour contributions, decide law cases and was responsible for the country's defence and foreign policies. Their offices were elective, with a state council, the Lhengye Tshogdu, electing the Desi for a period of three years.

FACING PAGE 77
For some young monk students both, bodhisattvas and football heroes, carry an enticing message from opposite directions beyond their monastery walls.

During his thirty-five-year reign, the Shabdrung (1616–51) and the first four Desi had to repulse several Tibetan and Mongol invasions. As the legends tell us, some were defeated by placing *thos*, heaps of stones that represented the Guardian Deities of the country, at certain spots while others were defeated with the help of a swarm of ravens who put the intruders to flight. The raven represents Legön Jaro Dongchen, a manifestation of Mahakala, the kingdom's protective deity. It still decorates the royal Bhutanese crown.

The Shabdrung died shortly after he retreated to the Punakha *dzong* to meditate to his death in 1651. For the sake of stability his death was concealed from the public until 1705, for over 50 years. Many of the feats of nation-building accorded to the Shabdrung were actually implemented by the first four Desi during this time. Until the beginning of the eighteenth century, the dual system of government worked well; subsequently, though, it led to two centuries of strife and civil wars over the question of power and succession.

In 1627, the first known Europeans reached Bhutan. Stephen Cacella and John Cabral were Portuguese Jesuit Priests on their way to Tibet. They offered the Shabdrung their services against the Tibetans, which he declined to accept. Their gifts, some guns and a telescope can still be seen in the Cheri monastery. By the end of the nineteenth century, the British had reached Cooch Behar, south of Bhutan and a mixed bag of relations that included several missions to the Bhutanese court focused on the control of the Duars, but eventually ended in an armed conflict. The British then annexed the Bengal and Assam Duars and the Treaty of Sinchula was signed in 1865, stipulating an annual

subsidy of Rs 50,000 to be paid to the government of Bhutan. Today, this treaty forms the basic framework for India's contribution to Bhutan's development, though the monetary amount involved has, of course, greatly changed.

IV

HEREDITARY
MONARCHY AND
GOVERNANCE

IN 1862, THREE YEARS BEFORE the Treaty of Sinchula between the British and the Bhutanese was signed, a son was born to Jigme Namgyel, the *Penlop* or governor of the province of Trongsa. His name was Ugyen Wangchuck, and he went on to become a man of destiny for Bhutan. As a descendant of two of the most respected lineages in Bhutan, he was also related to Pema Lingpa's family, settled in Kurtoe not far from Bumthang.

After more than two centuries of internal strife and the rule of fifty-four Desi (of which not a few died violent deaths), Bhutan still professed an unchanged lifestyle with a seemingly timeless Lamaist society. The Wangchuck dynasty was destined to change that and to bring Bhutan into the modern age. At the age of seventeen, Ugyen Wangchuck became the Penlop of Paro and shortly thereafter, in 1883, the Penlop of Trongsa. After defeating the Dzongpon (governor) of Wangdue Phodrang, even the Desi had to abide by the whims of the Trongsa strongman. In 1885 and after subduing a series of revolts, the decisive battle was fought at Changlimithang below Thimphu. The 4000-men strong Trongsa Penlop's troops routed the combined forces of Thimphu, Punakha, and Paro. Consequently, all of Bhutan once again came under one strong undisputed leadership, something that had not happened since the days of Shabdrung Ngawang Namgyal. Bhutan has not seen any internal rebellion, any warlike action since then.

To make sure that the Tibetan and Chinese influence

in the region did not become too strong, Ugyen Wangchuck maintained amicable relations with the British and even accompanied the expedition to Lhasa led by Francis Younghusband in 1904. For the British, a stable and strife-free Bhutan was an important asset along the Tibetan border. Finally, in 1907, Ugyen Wangchuck abolished the dual system of government and was elected as the hereditary monarch of Bhutan. The British envoy, Claude White, was present and said on the occasion: 'I am convinced that you have taken a wise step in thus consolidating the administration of the state. Sir Ugyen has been my friend for many years and you could not have made a better choice. His integrity, uprightness and firmness of character commend him to everyone …'

In hindsight, a century of peace, independence, stability, and slowly developing prosperity, without compromising the spiritual base of the country and the people, seem to confirm Claude White's words.

Within the Bhutanese society, there are several distinct classes that can easily be discerned. The royal family stands apart, though it does not stand outside the law. It is different for the King: Article 2/15 of the draft constitution says: 'The Druk Gyalpo shall not be answerable in a court of law for His actions and His person shall be sacrosanct.'

Before the advent of the hereditary monarchy, the Desi, the temporal heads of state, were elected for a limited time from among the Penlops, the regional

Created by the light of butter candles, the shadow of a praying novice mixes with a print of auspicious symbols.

PAGES 82/83
Nearly every man living in
Gantey is a Gomchen. While
they have professions and
work their fields, the monks
are supported by the religious
institution of the country.

governors, and the central body of monks. While the third Druk Gyalpo (Dragon King), Jigme Dorji Wangchuck, voluntarily made the conduct of the King answerable to the Tshogdu, the Bhutan National Assembly, he did not put kingship itself, the monarchy, at its disposal. In case of a vote of no confidence, which few Bhutanese could imagine, the crown prince or whoever was next in the line of succession, would automatically take his place. The King also surrendered his right to veto any law the Tshogdu passed.

Before the new 2008 constitution catapulted Bhutan into the twenty-first century, the King's powers were substantial. He was the highest moral and judicial authority, the highest Court of Appeal and the Commander-in-Chief of the armed forces. Even though kingship in Bhutan does not refer to a divine origin, the King was the temporal protector of the religion and the *sangha*, which is guided and controlled by the Dratshang, the central body of monks. The Druk Gyalpo also confirmed its head, the Je Khempo.

The fourth Druk Gyalpo, who brought all these changes to Bhutan, was and still is known to take his vow of 'Gross National Happiness' seriously and did not see it as a mere public relations stunt. His willingness to voluntarily give up most of his powers has few examples in history. When 'Gross National Happiness' as a government's political aim was first mentioned in a report in the *Financial Times* in 1987, it aroused considerable interest and curiosity. Bhutan's development since then has indeed confirmed that there is a substantial difference between the western focus on development and the Buddhism-based outlook the Bhutanese profess. For them, the spiritual, psychological, and ecological aspect of development is as important, if not more, than its economic content. Most of the royal family travels frequently into remote regions of Bhutan, which are only accessible by long foot marches, to get an independent assessment of the situation of people living in isolated mountains.

FACING PAGE 85
Seen all over Bhutan is the ubiquitous bright colour of the monks' robes. The gomchen, the Bhutanese lay priests, though, wear only a piece of red cloth over their *gho*s.

In past centuries, the question of succession was often a reason for incessant internal strife. Since the creation of the hereditary monarchy, that problem seemed solved, though the Shabdrung's Mind and Speech incarnations remained a factor of instability. Now, after King Jigme Singye Wangchuck married four daughters of Yab Ugyen Dorji, a nephew of the Sixth Mind incarnation, Shabdrung Jigme Dorji and brother of the late Sixth Speech incarnation, Chogley Jigme Tenzin, family feuds have become part of Bhutan's colourful though sometimes belligerent past.

Until the living content of the newly written constitution has taken roots in the country, Bhutan tries to overcome what so far has been missing in democratic terms by what is alluded to as the ancient Buddhist system of 'benevolent kingship'. With the solid Bhutanese and western education that the king received, the success of the evolving constitutional monarchy, where the people

The tsechu at the Gantey Gompa is one of the most mystical pageants in Bhutan. Most of the gompa's monks participate in one way or the other. Elder monks who cannot dance anymore prefer to be musicians.

FACING PAGE 88
What would seem like a
theatre costume in the west is
the everyday attire of senior
gelongs and lamas when they
come as spectators to the
annual *tshechus*.

PAGE 89
Pounding the drums is like
meditation for the musicians.
The long-reverberating
sounds ring on and help to
calm heightened emotions.

The masks that are worn
during the dance festivals and
the stories the dances tell,
revive animistic fantasies
and transform abstract
religious terms into a
palpable experience for
the senses.

Each step of the dancers of
Bhutan is choreographed.
Some of the dances originate
with Pema Lingpa, Bhutan's
foremost saint, who created
them in the sixteenth
century. Since then
professional dance masters
ensured they did not change
over time.

have the final say in their country's affairs, seems to depend only on the timely achievements in the educational, social, and economic sectors.

Remnants of the feudal structure of the old system are still visible. Traditionally, in the pageantry of religious festivals and rituals, the people's dress and conduct, and economically in the system of landownership. In medieval times, there were, and to a certain extent still are, two classes of peasantry. Those who owned land and houses and paid tax that constituted a certain percentage of the harvest plus manual labour (*khaip*), and the landless peasants (*drap*), who farmed the land of the *dzongs* and gompas on a crop-division basis. The third Druk Gyalpo, Jigme Dorji Wangchuck, who brought Bhutan into the twentieth century, changed this when he initiated land reforms in 1952 in the very first year of his reign. He put the ceiling of larger landholdings for individuals and religious institutions at thirty acres; at the same time, he also abolished serfdom.

Due to the high esteem accorded to saints and Rimpoches, and the two accepted lineages, the family lineage and the lineages of reincarnation, the Bhutanese are a rare example of a people aware of genealogies which often hark back to Tibetan clans and families who settled here as early as the twelfth century. The respect, regard and esteem for values embedded in these lineages are a telling feature of the social and spiritual lives of the people. Such reverence could not have survived if families with a rich heritage would not have been the stalwarts of religion, art and tradition over the centuries. These families, together with gompas and lhakhangs, are still principal landholders in the country. To what extent this elite will also occupy important positions in the evolving constitutional monarchy only history will tell. On the other hand, on the religious level, the system is transparent and permeable. The upward mobility within the religious system depends on spiritual awareness, intelligence, age, and pious conviction.

PAGES 92–95
Students watching a *tshechu* performance in the courtyard of the Gantey gompa. The dance festival is the annual highlight for the peasants of these remote mountains.

During medieval times, this had an important impact on the kind of feudalistic society that developed. Within the general public, there were few class distinctions, since the villages were self-sufficient. Besides farmers, most of them had their own carpenters, blacksmiths, masons, and woodcarvers. Money was unknown. Until half a century ago, taxes were still paid by labour and in kind, with grains, meat, butter, or livestock, which were then stored and distributed in the *dzong*s.

A law established by the fourth Desi at the end of the seventeenth century stipulated that in a family with three sons, the eldest inherited the land, the second became a monk, and the third had to become a government servant. The lamas of the well-organized central body of monks who controlled the country came mainly from the aristocracy, but also from the general

body of the population. If they left the *sangha* after their training, they could have families and political positions, but these were not hereditary, since except for the reincarnated Shabdrung, they were all elected, including the Desi.

The British envoy, George Bogle, who dealt with the Bhutanese in 1774 had this to say about their character and looks: 'The more I see of the Bhutanese, the more I am pleased with them. The common people are good-humoured, downright, and I think thoroughly trusty. The statesmen have some art which belongs to their profession. They are the best-built race of men I ever saw; many of them are very handsome, with complexions as fair as the French.'

Through modern secular education, a similar upward mobility has also developed in the ranks of present-day civil servants, but as already stated and similar to developed democracies in the west, members of the old families can be found in top posts in government. That is, however, self-explanatory, given the educational possibilities of times past. Modern Bhutan is still a very young nation, which until a short time ago had only one college, the Sherubtse College in Kanglung. The new Royal University of Bhutan, a federation of colleges and institutes, was inaugurated in June 2003 and Dasho Jigme Khesar Namgyal Wangchuck, while still the crown prince, became its Chancellor. Specialized education, though, is only available in India or elsewhere at foreign universities, something that only few families can afford. Grants from foreign institutions and government funds sponsor now the most brilliant students of every academic year.

As with the royal family, most of the aristocracy of Bhutan harks back to some of the great saints and lamas of the Drukpa or Nyingmapa sects. Before secular education was begun, any higher education was only transmitted in *dzong*s and lhakhangs, naturally connected with religious instructions. This kind of classic education, together with modern university degrees, is now the prerequisite for membership in today's elite class. It is also the source of Bhutan's unique traditional policies and the predominant world-view. In the past, Bhutanese who were educated abroad had to enter a mandatory 'reintegration course' upon their return if they wanted to enter public service. Even members of the royal family did so after returning from schooling in England. Everyone who enters the civil service today by passing the civil service examination is sent to villages for rural development studies lasting one or two months as part of their postgraduate course. Civil servants, on an average, are well versed in history and ancient traditions.

FACING PAGE 97
Due to the friendly relations between the Nyingmapas and the Kagyupas at the end of the seventeenth century, the Gantey gompa, the site of one of Bhutan's most colourful *tshechus*, was built like a *dzong*.

The Religious Establishment – Rimpoches, Lamas, Gelongs and Gomchen: Back in 1682, the fourth Desi, the last one who had both religious and temporal powers, made it compulsory for one of three sons in every family to become a monk. He reorganized the monastic order and gave it its enduring form by appointing four Lopons to assist the Je Khempo (head) in running the *sangha*. At that time, the monastic body consisted of 800 monks. Today, gelongs (ordinary monks), lamas and gomchen (lay monks) outnumber civil servants. About half of the roughly 7000 Bhutanese ordained gelongs and lamas are registered and receive a monthly subsidy from the state. There are another 15,000 gomchen who mostly belong to the Nyingmapa sect. They are lay monks, farmers, or artisans with families, who perform prayer ceremonies and propitiations in the remote villages.

Many of the monks are still novices or students, the playful young boys seen all over Bhutan who make their monk's robes appear like school uniforms; the others are fully ordained. As such, the latter have to live a celibate life, but can renounce their vow at any time for a set fine and are afterwards fully accepted in society and known as *gatey*.

Education in the monastery schools starts at an early age with years of

study in religious and professional arts. Once students are through with their basic studies, they often achieve proficiency in handicrafts, dancing, or painting, or become specialists in rhetoric, grammar, poetry, and religious philosophy, rituals and worship. The preparation of sacred food, the propitiation of evil spirits and the recitation by heart of the litanies is as important for their maturity as their more mundane accomplishments. A system of examinations controls their development and out of the body of ordained monks, the most able rise through the ranks.

Religious men in Bhutan come with different titles. Lamas are usually revered ordained monks (mainly in the upper hierarchy of gompas or lhakhangs), but can also be highly spiritual people, living an ordinary family life. It is the same with *tulkus* or Rimpoches (the great precious ones). They are reincarnations of saints or revered teachers. Since as small children they have been declared to be reincarnations, they will be seen and treated as *tulkus* all their lives. Besides their family lineage, they are seen to be reborn with the unimpaired karma and the spiritual capacity of their predecessor. There are also a few hundred white-clothed nuns, *anims*, in Bhutan, who, as in Theravada Buddhism, are subordinate to the monks.

To understand the deep devotion the populace has for people that take the spiritual path, one needs to know that only a practitioner who devotes his entire life to the *dharma* (moral law) can fully understand the profound aspects of the Buddha's teachings. Only then will he be capable of expounding them and practise the intricate and complex rituals. Mere scholarly studies will not suffice. Because of that, Bhutan is a country that has hermitages of every kind where practitioners and monks, as well as lay people, withdraw for different periods of meditation. The most esteemed of these is the 'three years, three months, three days' solitary retreat – a practice often followed in this country where spiritual gains are more important than mundane successes.

PRECEDING PAGES 98-99 AND 101
A class at the Trongsa *dzong*. Student monks study and pray from early morning until late evening. When necessary, teachers are stern and austere, though there is a predominant atmosphere of compassion.

FACING PAGE 100
The pages of religious books and the sacred texts are not only for the mind. For the pious, each leaf is precious truth that can be touched and felt by the hands.

The unequivocal support of the *sangha* mirrors the strong Buddhist conviction of the Bhutanese. In return, monks contribute to the well-being of the people at large with prayers, invocations, and rituals that often last for days. They create the ambience that allows the individual or household to influence the energies and powers – the deities and demons – they encounter in their daily struggles. Only spiritual masters, gelongs, lamas or gomchen who have received the appropriate initiations, explanations, and empowerment can perform these rituals. These initiations have been handed down in an unbroken line from the saints and founders of the different schools.

There are no begging monks in Bhutan. It is one of the duties of the state to make sure that monks can follow their studies, meditations, and rituals without having to worry about their corporeal needs. In Bhutan, the inner qualities of a man are seen as being as important for his well-being and society's stability as are economic factors. What distinguishes Bhutan from secular nations is the conviction that this can only be acquired through religious studies and practice.

The Tibetan social system of aristocrats and commoners entered Bhutan with its Tibetan immigrants. As in several places of Europe up to the eighteenth century, there was no division between spiritual and temporal powers. Unlike Europe though, the Himalayan aristocracy developed along two lineages, the family, and the reincarnation lineage that again produced a line of descent in the family lineages. Most saints, *tulkus* and Rimpoches had families and were involved in temporal matters of society, but it was their spiritual awareness that made them outstanding. Many Bhutanese thus can claim one of their ancestors being an important person in the spiritual transmission of their creed.

Since the ouster of the main body of monks from Tibet in 1959, many contemporary *tulkus* and Rimpoches, not only from Tibet, but also from Bhutan, have settled in western countries where they have a large following. They made true what Padmasambhava predicted in the eighth century: 'When the iron eagle flies and horses run on wheels, the *dharma* will go to the land of the red man.'

Now, with Tibet under Chinese occupation and Tibetan Buddhism in exile, Bhutan is the last haven where this thousand years-old religion still flourishes unhampered – protected by an entire nation. It is this what makes Bhutan so different from the rest of the world. The spiritual outlook on life has not changed. The actual semi-isolation of the country preserves what has disappeared elsewhere. Instead of entrepreneurial or political figures, royal patronage, and the devout populace still accord members of religious institutions central positions in society. Once physical survival is taken care of, the life of the average Bhutanese peasant is still focused on religion, its places of worship, and its rituals. They provide them with a raison d'etre, where western rationalism leaves a void.

FACING PAGE 103
As young people do everywhere, these young students love giggling and chasing each other along the many corridors of the Trongsa *dzong*.

The People – Peasants and Artisans: In pre-historic times, the indigenous population of Bhutan entered the foothills and valleys through the Duars in the south. They were an Australoid people that settled between the South China Sea and the Himalayas. They and Indo-Mongoloid people from the Brahmaputra valley ruled different parts of Bhutan up to the fifteenth century. They are now known as the Sharchops, the eastern people.

It was not until the ninth century that the Tibetans started to move southwards in large numbers. They call themselves Ngalops, which means 'the first converted', but in the past were also known as *Bhote*, the people who came from Bhotia or Tibet. They settled in western, central, and northern Bhutan and it was the meeting and mixing of the Mons, the Kochs, Khens, and the Ngalops that formed today's mainstream Bhutanese culture. While the animistic indigenous population added the heritage of their Bon religion, the Tibetans brought Tantric Buddhism. Together they produced Bhutan's unique religious and social fabric. People of Tibetan descent had already populated western Bhutan, since it was easily accessible from Tibet through the Chumbi valley. The inhabitants of the eastern provinces were Khens, Kochs, and Mons, who spoke Austronesian languages. Except for their language, their erstwhile differences have evened out over the centuries and today there are no ethnic or religious conflicts between them.

Besides the Ngalops and the Sharchops, there are also a few minor tribes in Bhutan. While the Brokpas are yak- and cattle-herders who live at high altitudes along the eastern border of Bhutan and wander between their summer and winter pastures, the Birmis are cultivators and producers of bamboo handicrafts. The Doyas live at low altitudes in the western Samtse district and are semi-nomadic cultivators who graze other people's cattle in the southern foothills. The Bodos came across the border in southeastern Bhutan, though they mainly live in Assam.

The last and not insubstantial group of Bhutanese, the Lhotshampas, the Bhutanese of Nepalese origin, make up about a quarter of Bhutan's population of approximately 650,000. They live predominantly in the south and have put the sincerity of the newly emerged nation and its Buddhist way of life to test because of the large numbers of people from the community that came swarming into Bhutan.

With the modernization of Bhutan's age-old government system and way of life, the problems of a modern nation state have rapidly surfaced. Nation-states are a recent feature in the development of political organization and have changed the self-image of its people. In times past, laws that were as old as Buddhist traditions or those devised by legendary Tibetan kings, were sufficient to govern the country. Today, ethnic and nationalistic ideas, unknown before, have to be taken care of. A formerly undisputed feudal system has to be converted into a socially viable polity that is globally compatible while being firmly based on Buddhist tenets.

FACING PAGE 104
The many courts, corridors and stairs in the Trongsa *dzong*, one of the largest in the Himalayas, are the playground and walkways for the students. The impressive structure helps to imprint solemnity and awe for their religion and culture in their still formative minds.

PAGE 106

Tamshing Lhakhang was founded by Pema Lingpa at the beginning of the sixteenth century. Here and at the Gantey gompa, Pema Lingpa's religious traditions have been followed strictly for half a millennium. Here his Mind and Speech incarnations are in the midst of a religious ceremony that lasts for several days.

PAGE 107

The head lama of the Trongsa *dzong* on his elevated seat in the great congregation hall. Only gelongs and students live within the mighty walls of the *dzong*, which they share during the day with the regional government. By sunset the doors close, then the *dzong* belongs again solely to the mendicants who are permitted to spend the night indoors.

When looking at contemporary Bhutanese society, many traits remain unchanged since the time when it was difficult to reach the Himalayan kingdom. Today, most Bhutanese are still peasants and artisans and neither their living conditions nor their mode of production has changed. Most villages are still as remote and almost as difficult to reach as hundred years ago. Air access to Bhutan through its only international airport in Paro was established in 1983, while television and the Internet came as late as 1999. The peasantry, which constitutes about eighty per cent of the population, is not much affected by these modern amenities.

Back in the seventeenth century, the Shabdrung had already installed the system of the thirteen arts and crafts, which also included paper-making, wood-turning, casting, goldsmith's work, weaving, stitching, bamboo work, painting, and pottery. It was a wise decision, since today these crafts can draw on centuries of experience that have not only flourished within the walls of the *dzongs*, but have also been handed down from mothers to daughters, from fathers to sons. Looms are still found in almost every household outside the cities and their products are often prized collector's items that take months to finish. The Sharchops of the east are known to be the best weavers of Bhutan, with every valley boasting of its own designs and pattern. Embroidery is also a traditional craft. Both weaving and embroidery are more than a just a pastime for the women in outlying villages since they earn additional income from their work. They refine their festival dresses, produce *thangkas* and scarves and assist the monks in making their colourful dancing costumes for the annual *tshechus* (religious festivals).

The Bhutanese are a sturdy people, living in joint family units of closely knit ethnic groups. They are not affluent, but poverty on the level of seasonal famines is unknown (some thirty per cent of the people earn less than the established national poverty line of Nu. 740 per month). For a people used to working hard, the land provides all they need for their sustenance. In the past, indebtedness of farmers, the curse of other parts of the developing world, was unknown since trade was based on barter of goods rather than on money. Cooperatives are now ensuring that debts do not slip in through the backdoor of material development.

FACING PAGE 109
Arts and crafts are an important part of a monk's education. In the seventeenth century, the Shabdrung, the nation's founder, installed the system of the thirteen arts and many monks practise one or more of them.

Semi-nomadic herders climb up the mountains to let their livestock graze on the lush vegetation and also take care of the cattle of lowlanders during summer. The power of water is harnessed to drive the village flourmills and also the prayer wheels that serve the spiritual needs of the community. Every village has a gompa, chorten, or lhakhang. Where there are no monks, gomchen, the local lay monks, perform *pujas* or prayer ceremonies, the year-round Buddhist rituals that are necessary to propitiate the spirits and local deities.

Due to the steep terrain, Bhutanese villages are built in

clusters on hill slopes surrounded by terraced and irrigated fields. Farmhouses are built with voluntary contributions of co-villagers and adhere to a similar design and layout. Animals are kept on the ground floor while the first floor comprises the living area with an open fireplace, but without a chimney. On this floor, we also find 'bedrooms' and the ever so important family shrine room or chapel. There are no stools, and rarely, a low table, while personal items are kept in chests and trunks. The top floor is reserved for keeping stores.

Pine slates secured with heavy stones protect houses against the regular after-noon winds that sweep through the valleys. During the dry season, the roofs are used to dry red and green chillies, their vivid colours brightening the landscape. Like the national dress code, Bhutanese architecture adheres to regulations that make it discernable from other architectural styles in the Himalayas. Elaborate wood-carvings on window

frames and protracted beams are found even in modest houses. The houses are still built with interlocking beams that support whitewashed walls of stone, hard packed mud or bricks. Glass is sparsely used; windows of a Bhutanese house usually have wooden shutters. In towns, the exterior of the houses have to abide by the national architectural building code, the interior depending on the economic status of the residents.

Until the 1960s, none of the Bhutanese community spaces could have been called a town. The hub of life was within the walls of the *dzongs* with regulated individual behaviour and an atmosphere befitting monastic premises. Even today, women are only permitted to enter a *dzong* during the day. When India's late prime minister, Indira Gandhi, visited the Trongsa *dzong* to stay there, she was made an an exception due to her position. The *dzongs'* huge and heavy wooden doors open at sunrise and are closed at sunset, after which only the residing monks are permitted to remain inside. Whoever enters a *dzong* is expected to wear his national dress and a ceremonial scarf that runs from the left shoulder underneath the right armpit and back to the left shoulder. Some of these scarves have a benedictory sentence printed on them, such as*: 'Blessed is the day; blessed is the night, midday is also blessed. May day and night bring the blessings of the Buddha, the Law and the Monk-body.'*

The doorways to Bhutan have opened only slightly and in 2007 not more than 17,000 western tourists visited the country, while very few Bhutanese have ever gone further than India. Only about forty years ago did the country emerge from within a cloak of medieval laws and customs, which, as in any society in transition, will take generations to change. Modern civil law is not always welcome, even though inevitable, by the traditional Bhutanese.

THE DRUK GYALPO
HIS MAJESTY
JIGME KHESAR
NAMGYAL WANGCHUCK

His Majesty the King, Jigme Khesar Namgyal Wangchuck, is the eldest of the fourth Druk Gyalpo's five sons and five daughters. After returning from his formal education in the United States and in England he became king at the age of twenty-six, when his father abdicated in his favour in December 2006.

ASHI TSHERING PEM WANGCHUCK,

ASHI DORJI WANGMO WANGCHUCK AND

ASHI TSHERING YANGDON WANGCHUCK

Their Majesties, Ashi Tshering Pem Wangchuck, Ashi Dorji Wangmo Wangchuck and Ashi Tshering Yangdon Wangchuck. His Majesty, the fourth Druk Gyalpo of Bhutan, is married to four sisters. Missing in this photograph is Her Majesty Ashi Sangay Choden who was visiting the United States when the photographs were taken. The queens are descendants of the family of Chogley Yeshey Ngodrup, the last Desi and fifth Speech incarnation and are related to both the sixth Mind incarnation and the sixth Speech incarnation of the *Shabdrung*.

DASHO UGYEN JIGME WANGCHUCK

His Royal Highness Dasho Ugyen Jigme Wangchuck, five, is the son of Her Majesty Ashi Tshering Pem Wangchuck. With ten children, of whom five are sons, this generation of the Wangchucks has no shortage of successors.

LYONCHHEN JIGMI YOSER THINLEY

His Excellency, the prime minister of Bhutan, Lyonchhen Jigme Y. Thinley. In the course of the reforms that further opened Bhutan to the rest of the world, he became prime minister twice and was later minister for home and cultural affairs during the reign of the fourth Druk Gyalpo. Bhutan has few foreign embassies, but since 1972, Bhutan is a member of the United Nations with bureaus in New York and Geneva, while several United Nations agencies have offices in Thimphu.

DASHO KARMA LETHO

Dasho Karma Letho, retired chairman of the Royal
Advisory Council and former Ambassador to India.
The Dasho and his wife, Aum Kinley Sedon,
are perfect examples of the Bhutanese gentry.
As in times past, they still feel responsible for the
spiritual well-being of the peasants working their
estates and spend time with them particularly
during *pujas* and rituals revolving round
the tutelary deities of their land.

JEKO TSHERING

Jeko Tshering, sixty-five, is formally still a monk of the Tashichodzong, where His Highness the Je Khempo resides, but due to his age, he retired for meditation to Hongtso, 20 kilometres from Thimphu. Throughout his life, he has spent long spells meditating as a recluse in remote monasteries.

LEKI SANGYE

Leki Sangye, fifty, is a Brokpa farmer and herder. His family of ten lives off his vegetable plots where he grows potatoes, radish, cabbage and spinach. In addition, he produces butter and cheese from forty yaks and sells the products at the market in Rangjung.

DEKI, DECHEN

Deki, nineteen, her sister Dechen, eighteen, with
their six-month-old babies, Tshering Norby and
Pasang Choden. Both Deki and Dechen cannot read
and write; Dechen went to school for just one
month. Brokpas purposely do not send some of their
children to school to make sure that there will be a
future generation of herders and farmers that will
stay on in their high-altitude environment. Few of
those who have continued schooling in the provincial
capital Trashigang have returned to settle
where they grew up.

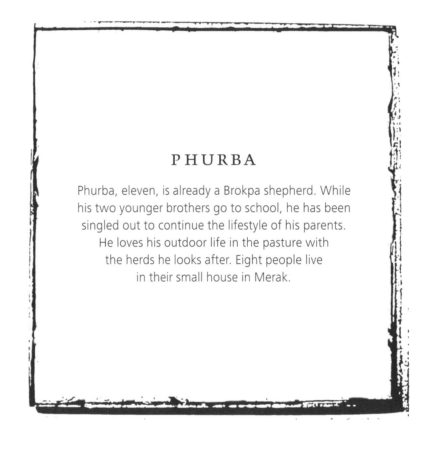

PHURBA

Phurba, eleven, is already a Brokpa shepherd. While
his two younger brothers go to school, he has been
singled out to continue the lifestyle of his parents.
He loves his outdoor life in the pasture with
the herds he looks after. Eight people live
in their small house in Merak.

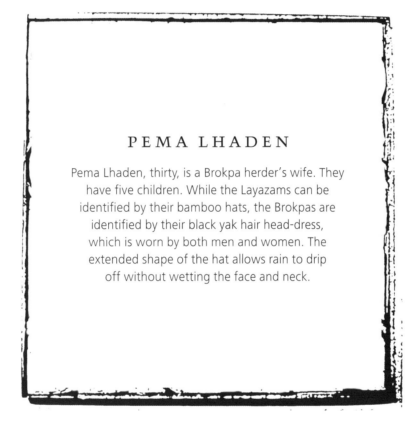

PEMA LHADEN

Pema Lhaden, thirty, is a Brokpa herder's wife. They
have five children. While the Layazams can be
identified by their bamboo hats, the Brokpas are
identified by their black yak hair head-dress,
which is worn by both men and women. The
extended shape of the hat allows rain to drip
off without wetting the face and neck.

LEKI THSERING

Leki Tshering, sixty-five, with his granddaughter Leki, three. Leki is a retired herder and farmer in Merak. He is the second-largest landowner in his village and pays an annual tax of 200 ngultrum for his land and house. He has eleven children and thirty grandchildren, his large family reflecting the population explosion resulting from the access to modern medicine. When he was born, there were just twenty-five houses in Merak and the now denuded hillsides were still heavily forested.

Before money was introduced in the 1960s, the staple food in this village was *tsampa*. But since they sell their cheese, yak butter and yak hair to traders from the valley, they can buy rice, which has now substituted *tsampa*. Leki has left his home in the eastern hills only once to visit Thimphu when he was twenty-eight years old.

TSITIM

Tsitim, sixty, is a Brokpa farmer who lives in Merak at an altitude of 4200 metres. She has three sons, one daughter and seven grandchildren. As several other regions southeast of Bhutan along the Indian border, Sakteng and Merak are still off-limits for foreigners and can only be visited with special permission. Nothing much has changed in the original lifestyle of the Brokpas. With their yaks, sheep and cows, which they move with the seasons, and their small vegetable plots they live self-sufficient lives on the upper line of human habitation in the Himalayas.

PHUNTHSO, NAMTSE

Phuntsho, twenty-five, and Namtse, thirty-nine. They are both cattle-herders, who move with their herds to higher pastures during the short summer. These pastures, which explode into exuberant vegetation once the snow has melted, are one of Bhutan's resources of wealth that would fall fallow if the traditional lifestyle of the Brokpa, Layops and other high-altitude herders would disappear. Brokpa never slaughter their cattle, though they kill yak and sheep for meat and leather. They also plant their own vegetables, but once in a while they hike down to the markets in Radi and Rangjung where they barter milk, butter and cheese for salt, oil, sugar, chillies, rice and household goods.

ZANGMO

Zangmo, thirty, and her husband are zomo breeders in Merak. A zomo is a cross between a yak and a cow. Zangmo and her husband own forty zomos, which can graze at higher heights and under colder climatic conditions than ordinary cattle.

TWO CONSORTS

Two consorts of Guru Rimpoche. Most of the Tantric saints were not celibate. They had several consorts, known in Sanskrit as *dakinis*. These female 'sky-goers', as they are called, have the power to arouse blissful energy in a man. Padmasambhava's best-known consort was Dakini Yeshe Tshogyal, who is known to almost every child growing up in the world of Tantric myths and is depicted in many *thangka* paintings. In religious terms, the *dakini* is to the saint what the muse is to the poet.

SAMGAN DORJI, SONAM, KINLEY TAWAD

Samgan Dorji, seventeen, Sonam, eighteen and Kinley Tawad, eighteen, monk-musicians at the Thimphu *tsechu*. During *tsechu*s, besides dictating the rhythm of the dance, it is their function to exhort the spiritual lineage – those who live in the Rabjam, the Heaven of the Ten Directions – to descend and assume the form of the dancers. Once that has happened, a dance performance is no more just a stage play; instead it brings the audience in direct contact with deities, spirits and saints.

GOMCHEN THUJI

Gomchen Thuji, sixty-two, has never been married, but
neither has he been an ordained monk. He is a
gomchen, one of the approximately 15,000 Bhutanese
lay priests who perform *pujas* and religious rites in
remote villages. Sowing and harvesting, as well as birth,
death and tri-monthly recitals are just a few of the
occasions when the populace get in touch with deities,
gods and guardians, the powers they strongly believe to
inhabit their world. The success of any of these rituals,
often conducted in the seclusion of private houses,
depends on the piety and the meditative power
of the performer and the hosts.

SANGAY WANGMO,
THUKTEN TSHERING

Sangay Wangmo, sixty-six, and Thukten Tshering, sixty-nine, are an elderly retired farmer couple from Shengang. They have seven children and live with their three sons who are in the army while the four daughters look after the farm. The tradition in central Bhutan is that the eldest daughter inherits the house and the fields. The husbands usually move into the houses of their wives and not vice versa. Sangay Wangmo and Thukten Tshering are typical of Bhutanese farmers who are strongly rooted in age-old traditions.

SONAM WANGYELWANG,
SINGAY NAMGAY

Sonam Wangyelwang, thirty, and Singay Namgay,
thirty-five, two modern Bhutanese men from Thimphu
in their ceremonial dress. It is worn whenever they are
on official business, when they enter a *dzong* and
during festivals. The quality of their *gho*s, the length
and cleanliness of their removable white cuffs and,
especially, the colour of their scarves are indicative of
their position in society. To be accepted in Bhutan,
fostering traditional Buddhist virtues is still a prerogative
for success. These virtues include an altruistic mind,
the control of anger, performing virtuous deeds,
the ability to concentrate, meditation and
the search for knowledge.

KINLEY DEMA

Kinley Dema, fifteen, is a high school student in
Thimphu. Teenagers in Bhutan, especially if they
attend high school, are all fluent in English. For
higher education, they can either continue their
studies at the Royal University of Bhutan,
which was founded in 2003 and comprises eight
member institutions, or go to foreign
learning institutes, mostly in India.

TANDIN WANGMO

Tandin Wangmo, sixty-seven, housewife in Thimphu.
While the majority of Bhutanese live in small hamlets
across the country, a rural exodus is already taking
place and Thimphu, the capital that not long ago had
only 15,000 inhabitants, will soon be a city of over
60,000. With the growth and modernization
of the city, changes in values and conduct are
taking place, changes that are still unknown
in the rest of the country.

A DANCER

A dancer holding the mask of the great saint Milarepa. This
mask is used in the dance 'The Stag and the Hounds', one of
the more popular performances during a *tsechu*. With
breaks, the dance lasts for three days and tells the story of
how the hunter and sinner Gonpo Dorji embraced dharma
after meeting Milarepa, the eleventh-century saint.
At one stage during the play Milarepa sings:

… your evil desires will never be quenched,
Instead, you will receive the blessings
If you give up your evil ways.
Outer appearances cannot be subdued
How much you may try,
It is now time to tame your inner mind.
Killing the stag will not quench your desires,
But killing the inner delusions
Will give you everlasting satisfaction …

TWO DANCERS

Two dancers with *atsara* masks. Religion is accorded
the highest esteem in Bhutan and no one is
permitted to mock Buddhism in public. That is, no
one except the *atsaras* during the *tsechu* dance
festivals. Here for once, the jesters can make jokes
about monks and religion. Within a traditional
framework of words and gestures, they crack jokes,
imitate the protagonists and assume funny postures
while a serious story is told. *Atsaras* bring a
lively element into the dances. These jesters
endear themselves to children who tire easily
when the dances drag on for too long without
the clowns appearing.

CHIMI DORJI, PEMA TSHERING AND NORBU GYELTSEN

Chimi Dorji, Pema Tshering and Norby Gyeltshen, all seventeen years old, are students at Thimphu's Junior High School. They are students with an excellent academic record whose future jobs will most probably be with the government. With few promising opportunities in the private sector, careers in the government are the preferred choice of graduates. For these jobs, however, they must be steeped in traditional Bhutanese values, which start with individual self-discipline and end with a responsibility towards all sentient beings. In practice, this inculcates an exceptional ecological awareness in government officers and citizens.

MONKS

Monks dressed as wrathful or terrifying Deities. The
Tungam dance of the Terrifying Deities has a deep
symbolic meaning. It harks back to the time of
Guru Rimpoche. To a Tantric Buddhist it is known
that there are evil men and demons that cannot be
converted by peaceful means. To save them,
nevertheless, Guru Rimpoche appears in the form of
the 'Fierce Thunderbolt', holding the *phurbu,* the
ritual dagger, and kills them in a dramatic whirl. By
doing this, he not only saved the world, but also
liberated the perpetrators of evil. In spite of the
drama and the ritual murder, which seemingly does
not fit into Buddhist philosophy, the message of this
dance is compassion and has a positive tone. It
shows that even the ignorant evil-doer has a
chance to be released from his sins.

SONAM JAMSO

Sonam Jamso, twenty-seven, is a folk dancer. In this dance, the Polay Molay, he wears the mask of a princess. The dance tells a story that harks back to the ancient Indian kingdom of Ngaden. The story reveals an underlying truth of Buddhism that eternal happiness is not found in mundane love, but only in the Triple Jewel – the 'Three Precious Ones', the Buddha, the Law and the Sangha. During *tsechu*s three different classes of dancers perform – monks who live in the *dzongs*, lay dancers from the villages and folk dancers who are employed by the national government.

DAGO

Dago, seventy, is a gold- and silversmith in Thimphu. He was born, and spent all his life, in Thimphu. He is married and has three children. He proudly told us that he had 'flirted' with about 300 girls in his life. Dago is not very religious. In Tantric Buddhism, it is the sublimation and even the experiencing of passion, not its suppression, that often puzzle the uninitiated. For lay townspeople who follow a mundane course of life, there are five Buddhist precepts, the *domba nga*. Bhutanese abide by them in the same way as the average Christian follows the ten commandments. For a Mahayana Buddhist this means: not killing; not taking what is not given to them rightfully; not lying; avoiding sexual misconduct and not consuming intoxicants.

YANGKHU

Yangkhu, thirty-five, is the driver of the former home minister. He is a very religious man as can be seen by the hardened point on his forehead. It comes from countless prostrations in front of religious images in lhakhangs or temples across the country. He is married, has three children and is a perfect example of the mixture of traditional and modern lifestyles that makes Bhutan unique. When driving, he would never bypass a *chorten* or a *mani* wall on the right side, even if the road was bumpy and had potholes; he would pass it in the same direction as when circumambulating them in prayer. Having traversed every motor road in Bhutan, he knows almost every sacred rock and religious structure and their mythical significance.

PEMA DENTRUP

Pema Dentrup, fifty-seven, is a traditional carpenter. He was born in Lingshi and for ten years was a monk at the Lingshi *dzong*. At the age of thirty-four, he left the *sangha* and became an apprentice to a carpenter. He never went to any government school, but knows how to read, write and calculate. In his twenty-three years of professional life, he has built nineteen houses without using any machinery. Everything, from the cutting of planks and logs is still done by hand. No nails or iron cleats are used to strengthen the wooden structures of the houses and the roof timbering. It is the traditional artistry of specialists like Pema Dentrup that give Bhutanese villages their particular unique appearance. A national building code makes sure that the traditional architecture of Bhutan remains a living art and distinguishes Bhutanese houses from the rest of the Himalayan buildings. Thus, Pema Dentrup contributes to the preservation and creation of a distinctive Bhutanese identity.

ONGMO

Ongmo, twenty-five, and her six-year-old child. She
lives in Laya, not far from the Tibetan border. While
her husband is a horse driver who transports goods
between their village and Punakha, she works the
family fields. Ongmo has been married for seven
years and has two children.

DORJI

Dorji, thirty, the outgoing *gup* (headman) of Laya. Even before the new democratic direct election of headmen became law in 2003, Dorji was already chosen by public suffrage. He studied three years at the Laya monastery and has been to almost every large town in Bhutan. To make sure that the mule track that connects Laya with the outside world stays in order, every family has to provide one person every year to work for fifteen to thirty days for this or other public work projects. This type of 'working tax' is equally applicable to men and women. Since 1993, women are paid the same amount of money as men. The *gup* selects them and pays them 100 ngultrum per day if it is a public job not directly connected with the needs of the village.

TENZIN

Tenzin, sixty, is a farmer and herder. The logs he
provides and transports, serves as fuel both for
cooking and heating at the village school. Except for
travelling once to Paro and Thimphu, he has not been
away from Laya. While he never attended school,
two of his six children have.

LHADEN

Lhaden, thirty, is a shopkeeper in Laya. She is a very enterprising woman. She owns four shops where she sells groceries, liquor and small household items. Even though there are many modern Chinese goods available across the border in Tibet, none of them can be sold at this remote Bhutanese outpost. Most of the modern hardware goods she sells in her shop come all the way from India – by lorry to Punakha and then on horseback to Laya. Lhaden also owns two houses, five cows and several fields where she grows barley and buckwheat. Her husband is a horse driver who owns eight horses and transports her goods to and from the nearest road point on the feeder road to the highway – a three-day downhill trek.

LEKI WONKCHUK, LEKI AND DORJI WONGCHUK

Leki Wonkchuk, seven, Leki Wongchuk, ten, and Dorji Wongchuk, eleven. All the three boys go to school. There are five grades in the school at Laya and a further three grades in the school at Gasa, a day's walk away from Laya. They are still children and pupils, yet they already help in the fields and in grazing yaks during vacation time. In remote regions like the Bhutanese Himalayas, child labour has a totally different connotation than in a modern urban environment.

TSHEWANG AND TINLEY

Tshewang, twenty-three, and Tinley, twenty-six. Both
are ex-monks from Laya. Now they are called *gatey*
and perform necessary *pujas* in the village. While
Tshewang was a monk for seven years in Simthokha
and Gasa, Tinley followed that vocation for ten years
in Laya. Now, after receiving a basic training at the
Gasa hospital for three months, he is the official
public health worker of the village. Both of them are
not married and live with their parents' families.
If they marry, they will move their wives
to their parents' house.

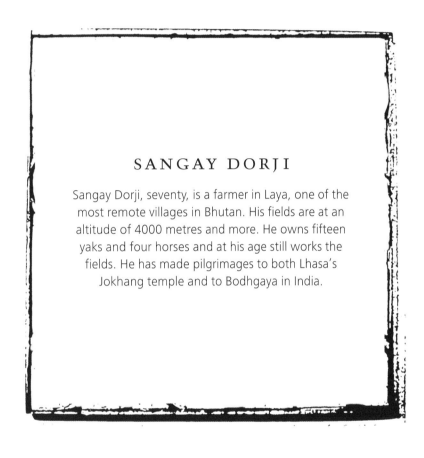

SANGAY DORJI

Sangay Dorji, seventy, is a farmer in Laya, one of the most remote villages in Bhutan. His fields are at an altitude of 4000 metres and more. He owns fifteen yaks and four horses and at his age still works the fields. He has made pilgrimages to both Lhasa's Jokhang temple and to Bodhgaya in India.

DORJI WANGMO

Dorji Wangmo, eighty, is the oldest person in Laya.
From age six to age eighteen she lived as a nomad,
moving constantly with a herd of yaks, living year in
and year out in a black yak felt tent away from any
village. At the age of eighteen, she got married and
moved to her husband's farm. Her husband died
thirty-three years ago. Of her eight children, only
three survived. She has eleven grandchildren
and two great-grandchildren.

V

PRESERVING A UNIQUE
IDENTITY: MODERN
BHUTAN

BHUTAN IN THE TWENTY-FIRST CENTURY, led in the crucial years up to 2008 by its vigorous, traditionally and western educated fourth Druk Gyalpo (the King of the Dragon Country), King Jigme Singye Wangchuck, tries to preserve and combine an unbroken spiritual tradition, a pristine environment, and modernization at a pace that follows a different tune. The monarch expressed the goal succinctly: 'Instead of putting the Gross National Product at the centre of our endeavours, let us strive for Gross National Happiness.'

In the Bhutanese-Tantric context, this includes all of living nature. Compassion for all creatures and not only for fellow men thus becomes the characteristic of the country and its people. It goes beyond what the Bhutanese definitely need to preserve, situated as they are between India and China, the two most populous nations in the world: their unique national identity. Within the last fifty years, they have seen two of their once independent neighbors, Tibet and Sikkim, being integrated into these mighty secular entities. They know they can be spared a similar fate only by a combination of invigorating their unique culture and by modernizing sensibly.

The Bhutanese concept of their identity relies emphatically on their spiritual heritage; it differs profoundly from their secular neighbours' and is a far cry from the economic and politically determined approach of our time. While elsewhere nations strive for a better future with might and power, Bhutan comes with a voice that needs to be heard by a world that seems to have lost the capacity to cross the confines of positivisms.

Since the creation of the monarchy and the abolition of the dual system of government, Bhutan, then still an absolute monarchy, has turned from an isolated country with a medieval feudal economic and political structure into a modern nation state with democratic institutions.

Sir Ugyen Wangchuck died in 1926 and his son, Jigme Wangchuck, became – as it was seen during British times – the King of Bhutan, his reign lasting until his death in 1952. India, in the meantime, had become independent. After negotiations India returned Deothang (Dewangiri), held until then by British India, to Bhutan. The new treaty contained provisions from the Treaties of Sinchula and the 1910 Treaty of Punakha, but was clearly between two sovereign nations, and the King of Bhutan was mentioned for the first time in an international document as the Druk Gyalpo.

Even though Bhutan wished to have good relations with both its neighbours, Tibet and India, one article in the treaty stated that Bhutan would be guided by India in its external affairs. The working bi-lateral Indo-Bhutanese understanding, though, was based on Bhutan's sovereignty. Since then and in the light of the changes taking place in Bhutan, the revised friendship treaty of February 2007 removed some obsolete provisions and focused on consolidating and expanding economic cooperation.

The next Druk Gyalpo, Jigme Dorji Wangchuck, initiated the changes that permanently ended the geographic and political isolation of the country. Roads were rapidly built, a barter economy was changed into a money economy, serfdom was abolished, and a base of indigenous, trained administrators, and educators started to be established. He set up a National Assembly, the Tshogdu, separated the judiciary from the executive branch of government, and abolished capital punishment. To bring Bhutan onto the road of a constitutional monarchy, he set an unparalleled example by subjecting the monarch to a vote of confidence every three years by the National Assembly. In 1971, the most important step regarding its identity in a world of independent nations was accomplished: Bhutan became a member of the United Nations. In 1972, the King died prematurely at the age of forty-four and was succeeded by his then seventeen-year old son Jigme Singye Wangchuck. Like his father, the new King too, was educated in Bhutan and abroad, in India and in England.

For a country like Bhutan that had a self-sufficient economy and a concept of feudal justice and equality determined largely by its spiritual and religious tradition, the integration into a global community was and is not easy to accomplish. A series of five-year plans that started in 1961 with the help of the Indian Planning Commission took care of socio-economics and drew heavily on the generation of ecologically 'clean' hydroelectric power that is now exported to India and, under changed conditions, could one day even energize the industrial development of the arid Tibetan plateau.

The appearance of an urban middle class, tourism, and a rise in the number of Bhutanese being educated abroad, have changed the expectations of the educated class, and is changing the outlook of a historically hardy people that still live in isolated villages. Bhutan is now connected through radio, television, telephone, and Internet with the outside world and with ideas that are often as strange to some of the villagers as the worship of guardian demons is for the purely materialist.

In 1975, shortly after the then young monarch ascended the throne, Bhutan was shocked by the abolition of the more than 300-year old monarchy in Sikkim. The Chogyal was ousted following a plebiscite in which the Hindu-Nepalese majority outvoted the Sikkimese Buddhist minority and Sikkim consequently became the twenty-second state of India.

PAGE 187
Goods that can be purchased in this Paro shop are often pure luxury for most peasants and herders. Until 40 years ago there was no money in circulation. Goods were acquired by barter.

A similar situation, resulting in severe ethnic confrontations and political instability, could be envisioned in Bhutan. The demographic situation, especially in southern Bhutan, had dramatically changed over the last century with the arrival of Hindu immigrants from Nepal (Lhotshampas). Liberalization measures in the 1970s encouraged intermarriage and provided opportunities for public service for the Lhotshampas, but the situation remained critical. Thus, to ensure that the country's religious and cultural identity was not watered down, the government started its programme of 'Driglam Namzha' (the common Bhutanese social etiquette and code of conduct), which prescribed the compulsory wearing of a national dress and removed the Nepali language from the school curriculum. At the beginning of the 1990s, those Nepalese who could not prove to have been in Bhutan by 1958 had to leave the country. The creation of a common Bhutanese identity, shared by all, had become a pressing internal objective of the government.

A series of steps towards the democratization of the

country was also implemented. In 1998, the King gave up his role as the head of government and appointed a prime minister and in 2002, Bhutan held its first election. It was not yet for the unicameral Tsoghdu, but for the position of the *gups*, the village headmen. This pointed the way to further radical changes.

While the National Assembly consisted of 150 members, a council of ministers and a royal advisory council, the King set up a committee that was to draft a modern constitution. Thirty-nine members, headed by the chief justice, studied the constitutions of fifty countries for four years, before presenting the outcome of their deliberations to the King who then floated it in March 2005 to the public to study it and eventually vote on it. A penal code and an evidence act based on forgiveness and rehabilitation were also drafted. Symbolically, it should reflect the High Court's crest, a golden yoke, tied with a white silken knot, that can be loosened.

The third draft constitution published in August 2007 was to end a century of absolute power for the Bhutanese Kings. Accepted by the people, it replaces the royal decree for the constitution of the National Assembly of 1953, which initiated the modernization of the country and brought Bhutan into the modern world. The 2008 constitution, replacing the monarchy with parliamentary democracy, finalizes the modernization of the country. Bhutan has arrived in the contemporary world. It has become an example to prove that changes, as profound as in Bhutan, affecting the very lives of its citizens, can be accomplished without civil wars and internal upheavals.

Another development that also influenced the speed of change in Bhutan was the King of Nepal's action in 2005.

Due to seemingly insoluble social problems, King Gyanendra of the neighbouring country dissolved the parliament, dismissed the government and usurped power in what was seen as a 'royal coup'. Within a short period, this resulted in the loss of power of the Nepalese royal house.

King Jigme Singye Wangchuck announced that free elections would take place in 2008, which consequently would result in Bhutan becoming a constitutional monarchy with parliamentary-democratic structures. He also announced his abdication and the enthronement of the crown prince, Jigme Khesar Namgyal Wangchuck, as the country's fifth Druk Gyalpo.

PAGE 189
In Mahayana Buddhist philosophy manifestations of a saint can surface again in a reincarnation. Thus, his teachings are carried into the future. Three emanations of Pema Lingpa, Bhutan's foremost Terton, can be experienced and venerated by the public in the persons of the body incarnation, the mind incarnation and the speech incarnation.

Modernizing a country, whose highly evolved social and religious system has not changed much within the last thousand years, without destroying a way of life that contains exemplary traits of human interaction, is a sensitive undertaking that required a cautious approach. In 'Bhutan 2020', the development mission statement of the Bhutanese government says: 'Our approach to development has been shaped by the beliefs and values of the faith we have held for more than 1000 years. Firmly rooted in our tradition of Mahayana Buddhism, the approach stresses not material rewards, but individual development, sanctity of life, compassion for others, respect for nature, social harmony, and the importance of compromise. … (we want) to draw upon and conserve this rich fund of social and cultural philosophy to achieve a balance between the spiritual and material aspects of life.'

The only way in which this statement differs from the social aspect of what Buddha Shakyamuni preached is the modern language, proving that certain truths have a timeless ring.

KUENZANG PEMA NAMGYAL RIMPOCHE

9th Body Incarnation

TEMPEY GYELTSEN

10th Mind Incarnation

JUNGDREL KUENZANG RANGDREL

11th Speech Incarnation

ACKNOWLEDGEMENTS

It is now more than twenty years since we actively started this endeavour, a quest that will not end for the rest of our lives. It is a search for visible signs of the ephemeral raison d'être, as it is engraved on the diverse faces of living humanity.

In the course of these twenty years, we have met many people who have contributed in one way or another, directly or indirectly, to the making of this book. They are fellow citizens of the twenty-first-century, tribals, craftsmen and academicians, from all continents. Slowly, many of them may vanish from our memory. It is their photographs and their ideas, which we brought back that will stay with us. Our foremost gratitude goes to them.

The first book in this ongoing project, *In Search of Dignity*, acquainted the reader with people who still believe in the Mother Goddess, in a supreme world ruler, in saints and prophets or simply in nature spirits – some had no religious belief at all. We knew we had to follow it up with a focused visual study of one country and we decided to do that in Bhutan, in the last Mahayana kingdom on the face of the earth.

To move portable studio, measuring 8 by 4 by 4 metres, across the Himalayas was no mean task, one that could not have succeeded without the dedicated assistance of local Bhutanese who saw the value in what we were doing, who saw that our time is one of great change and that there is something precious in danger of vanishing that needs to be preserved for generations to come. It was Dasho Karma Letho, the retired Chairman of the Royal Advisory Council who understood this. He and the then Foreign Minister of Bhutan, Lyonpo Jigme Thinley, opened most of the doors that otherwise would have remained closed to us, as the entire country and its lifestyle is still shrouded in mystery for many western visitors. The same must be said of Dasho Sangey Wangchuk, the Secretary of the Special Commission on Cultural Affairs. They and the respective *Dzongdags* in the different regions, which we visited, gave us all the assistance we needed. They permitted us to photograph inside *dzongs* and lhakhangs that do not solicit foreign visitors and permitted us to hike to off-limit regions where yak-herders still live in an ever-unchanged pastoral fashion.

But there were also others – the many sincere, affectionate and unbelievably sturdy Bhutanese who accompanied us on our week-long treks across the mountains, the translators, guides, the car- and horse-drivers and porters without whom we would never have been able to move nearly a ton of equipment into camps at altitudes of 4000–5000 metres. Yangkhu, Tashi, Dawa and Sonam, just to mention four of them, taught us more about the Bhutanese than we have learned from books. And they made us aware of the bright intelligence these Himalayan people possess.

Then there was Renate, who vigorously hiked across 4500-metre-high passes with us to note down what the people whom we photographed had to tell us about their lives and in addition took care that we did not have to survive only on *tsampa* and buttered tea and Tim, Günter's son, who as his assistant made his first field trip into one of the remotest regions of the world. At home were Pia and Sabine who made sure that our urbane lives, the studio and the family were not totally abandoned during our months' long absence.

Our gratitude also goes to Sonam Kinga, the well-travelled Bhutanese scholar who gave us invaluable hints and corrected us whenever our western perspective became too dominant. The same gratitude goes to Chambula Dorji who not only provided a home for us in Thimphu, but helped wherever he could, and to our friends in India, the UK and Germany who knew more about the country than we did and critically accompanied every step of our quest.

PAGE 191
The portable studio during the annual tshechu in the courtyard of the Tashichoedzong in Thimphu.

Günter Pfannmüller
and Wilhelm Klein
Frankfurt / Koh Samui

BROKPAS
yak- and sheep-herders of Tibetan descent who live at high altitudes on the border with Arunachal Pradesh.

CHORTEN
also known as *stupa*, Buddhist monument.

DASHO
equivalent to the English 'Sir' and meaning 'the best' in *Dzongkha*. At official gatherings, those bestowed with this title by the king wear a red scarf and a sword.

DRUK GYALPO
the King of the Dragon Country.

DZONG
fortress that houses both the administration and the district's monastic community.

GELONG
a fully ordained monk, also called *Lopen* or *Lam*.

GELUGPA
the Lamaist sect, best known worldwide as 'Yellow Hats', whose spiritual head, the Dalai Lama, is seen as a reincarnation of *Avalokiteshvara*.

JE KHEMPO
the spiritual head of the *Drukpa Kargyupa*, the National Church of Bhutan.

MAHAYANA BUDDHISM
its meaning in Sanskrit is the 'Greater Vehicle' in contrast to *Hinayana*, the 'Lesser Vehicle'. Mahayana Buddhism emerged around the first century AD. Mahayanists attribute an unearthly quality to the Buddha and see the historical Buddha as an earthly manifestation of the celestial Buddha.

MANTRA
a sacred utterance that helps concentration and is considered to possess mystical or spiritual efficacy.

NGALOPGS
meaning 'the first converted'.

PADMASAMBHAVA
known as Guru Rimpoche, the eighth-century saint who brought Buddhism to Tibet and Bhutan.

SAMSARA
the indefinitely repeated cycles of birth, misery, and death caused by karma.

SANGHA
the Buddhist monastic order.

TANTRA
means 'fabric' in Sanskrit and points to the interconnectedness of all things.

THERAVADA
the conservative branch of Buddhism adhering to the original Pali scriptures and the nontheistic ideal of Nirvana for a limited select number of adherents.

TSHECHU
religious festival in honour of Guru Rimpoche.

TSHOGDU
the National Assembly.

TULKU
reincarnation of a religious master, also called Rimpoche.

ISBN: 978-81-7436-678-8

© Roli & Janssen BV 2008
Published in India by
Roli Books in arrangement with
Roli & Janssen BV, Netherlands
M-75 Greater Kailash II Market
New Delhi-110 048, India
Ph: ++91-11-29212271, 29212782, 29210886
Fax: ++91-11-29217185
E-mail: roli@vsnl.com
Website: rolibooks.com

Original German edition published at Frederking & Thaler Verlag
© Frederking & Thaler Verlag, München 2006 -
www.frederking-thaler.de <http://www.frederking-thaler.de>

Photographer: Günter Pfannmüller, Frankfurt
Text: Wilhelm Klein, Koh Samui

Editor: Simar Puneet
Layout: Naresh L Mondal
Production: Naresh Nigam, Kumar Raman

Printed and bound in Singapore